Fee
Way ...

MW01104598

A Practical Guide for Working with Emotional Experience

Sibylle Artz
Assistant Professor
School of Child & Youth Care
University of Victoria
Victoria, British Columbia

Trifolium Books Inc.
Toronto

Trifolium Books Inc.

238 Davenport Road
Suite 28
Toronto, Ontario M5R 1J6
Canada

ISBN 1-895579-34-1

This material has been developed as part of the Career Counselling Training Project (CCTP). The CCTP is funded by the Canada Employment and Immigration Commission, the British Columbia Ministry of Advanced Education, Training and Technology, and the University of Victoria. CCTP is a project administered under CAMCRY and the Canadian Guidance and Counselling Foundation, Ottawa, Ontario, Canada.

Canadian Cataloguing in Publication Data

Artz, Sibylle, 1949-
    Feeling as a way of knowing: a practical guide
    for working with emotional experience.

Includes bibliographical references and index.
ISBN 1-895579-34-1

1. Emotions.   2. Counseling.   I. Title.

BF531.A77 1994   152.4   C93-095120-4

Design/desktop publishing: Rick Eskins
Editing/production: Francine Geraci
Illustrations: Cat Sullivan

Printed in Canada at Webcom

Last digit is print number: 9 8 7 6 5 4 3 2 1

Dedication

This book is dedicated to Joan Krisch, one of the founding members of the Bridges Project, who uses feeling as a way of knowing, and lives life to its fullest.

Foreword

Historically, emotions have been associated with the more primitive and base aspects of human nature. In English-language cultures especially, negative emotions have been treated as offensive and not to be tolerated, and even positive emotions have been subject to regulation by moderation and propriety. Folk language offers numerous models for controlling emotional feelings: "Big boys don't cry" and "only naughty girls get angry with their mothers" are just two such examples.

In early psychological history, such writers as Freud, James, and Dewey gave great attention to emotionality. With the emergence of behaviorism early in this century, emotion as an object of scientific interest nearly drifted into oblivion. For a time, some psychologists even believed that emotion as a term would eventually disappear. Phenomena once covered by the term emotion would be relegated to physiology, either as "hard-wired" instinctual impulses or "spillover" from nervous activity.

Under the influence of humanistic psychology, Gestalt therapy, and various neobehavioral or cognitive behavioral psychotherapies as well as psychodynamic therapies, the role of emotion re-emerged as extremely important in human interaction. Unfortunately, considerable emphasis continued to be placed upon the view that emotion was something to be controlled, re-directed, or moderated. For example, "corrective emotional experience" was held by some to be the most important ingredient in successful counselling and psychotherapy. In other words, even the humanistic therapies have continued to emphasize rational control over emotional processes, viewing emotion mainly as a liability and an obstacle to growth and healthy living.

Recent studies have cast emotion and feelings in a different light. It is now widely accepted that emotional processes are extremely powerful in directing attention, and are profoundly involved in acts of perception, memory, and learning. The expressive aspects of emotion are seen as important factors in interpersonal communication and in such basic processes as bonding. How we experience emotional feelings is part of how we develop a sense of self. In short, emotions are increasingly construed as important, constructive elements in ways of knowing self, others, and the world. Instead of asking, "How can we control emotions?" current thinking in psychology points to the question, "How can we learn to use emotions as an important medium for expanding our ways of knowing self, situation, others, and world?"

Sibylle Artz has written an important guidebook for practicing counsellors, child and youth care workers, social workers, and other professionals who wish to help their clients use emotional experience as a way of knowing. This book provides a conceptual introduction to the importance of working with emotions as a potential form of knowing. It also provides a Six-Step Strategy for "unpacking" the meanings embedded in emotional experience and for understanding the importance, meaning, and value of specific emotional experiences. The strategy can be used with individuals or in a group. Clients introduced to the Six-Step Strategy not only develop a better understanding of their present emotional experience, but gain a more extensive vocabulary for use with future emotional experience. As I read this book, it occurred to me that here is an educational method for helping people to increase their "emotional intelligence"!

R. Vance Peavy

Preface

When I began the work that led to the articulation of the ideas in this book, my own attempts at teaching survivors of abuse to engage productively and positively with their own and others' emotional experiences had foundered on the shoals of commonly used teaching and counselling approaches to emotion. At that time, most such approaches appeared to be concerned with the achievement of emotional stability. They suggested (and still suggest) that the quickest route to this desired end is through catharsis — the reduction of an impulse or an emotion through direct or indirect expression — followed by management of emotional experience through the application of strategies for emotional control. However, my students (participants in the Bridges Project, a federally funded program for adult female survivors of abuse) resisted these notions.

Two things were happening. Firstly, catharsis was not taking place. Instead, the expression of feelings seemed to trigger more feelings among members of the group, leading to a collective escalation in the level of emotional intensity. Secondly, most participants complained that the emotional management techniques suggested by their texts (techniques designed and recommended by cognitive therapists who claim that negative emotional experience is the result of faulty thinking) left them feeling guilty and inadequate. The emotional climate in the classroom was rapidly deteriorating, and emotional experience as a topic for study was not popular. This failure prompted me to seek a new approach to the situation.

Thus far I had relied upon approaches that treat feelings and emotions as reactive expressions leading to behavioral problems in need of control. That was precisely the problem. As I surveyed the situation in my classroom, I realized that my students wanted to treat their feelings as something other than mere behavioral problems for which they were responsible because of their faulty thinking. I also saw that my students were clever enough to demonstrate to me directly what research had also indicated. For while some theorists still believed in the cleansing power of catharsis, others have shown quite conclusively with both children and adults that rather than reducing feeling, expression heightens and increases it (Buss, 1966; Loew, 1967; Nelsen, 1969). Neither expression of feeling nor the identification of faulty thinking appeared to offer much therapeutic value.

I turned back to my students and listened carefully to their assessment of the situation. As they expressed their needs with regard to emotional experience, I heard what emerged as a theme. They wanted neither to be pumped and pressured to expose their emotions, nor did they want their emotional experience to be analyzed and regulated. They wanted to be understood. This prompted me to turn to sources outside the more conventional approaches to counselling in order to find other ways to work with emotion.

The theorists I looked to for greater insight into feeling began their own work with a desire to understand emotion rather than to regulate and control it, which was where my students and I also wished to begin. Among these theorists was Robert Solomon (1983), who suggested that "emotions are not disruptions or irrational occurrences, not forces or feelings or mere tendencies to behave. . . . Through our passions we constitute our [subjective] world, render it meaningful and with it our lives and our Selves" (p. 179). Solomon views our emotions as "our own and our own doing." He concurs with other philosophers and thinkers, who come mostly from outside the realm of modern psychology, when he says that emotions are judgments, evaluations, interpretations — ways of knowing and understanding ourselves and our world. This premise became the starting point for my own work with emotion. I moved from treating feeling as reaction and expression to working with feeling as a way of knowing, a psychological process that helps us to make sense of experience.

In order to work with feeling in this way, I learned how and why we commonly approach feeling and emotion in the ways that we do; researched ways of knowing and developed an approach to feeling that respected individual differences in emotional experience; and created a simple strategy for uncovering the knowledge embedded in our feelings. This book is the result of that undertaking. It offers a simple, straightforward, and practical approach to emotional experience that allows the feeling person to work with emotion rather than against it.

Sibylle Artz
Assistant Professor
School of Child & Youth Care
University of Victoria
Victoria, British Columbia

Acknowledgments

This book could not have been written without the participation and goodwill of many people. I wish to acknowledge and thank Dr. Vance Peavy for encouraging me to undertake this project and for his guidance, support, and practical help at each step along the way. I wish to thank Valerie Ward from the Canadian Guidance and Counselling Foundation for her invaluable editorial help, and I want to express my gratitude to Cathie Walker, secretary for the School of Child and Youth Care, University of Victoria, for her careful attention to every detail of this book.

Great appreciation and thanks are also due to the staff and students of the Bridges Project for giving me the room to work with them on creating the strategies and understandings described here.

Lastly, my thanks to Trifolium Books and my editor, Francine Geraci, for bringing this project to publication.

Contents

Introduction

Feeling, emotion, passion: this is the "stuff" of everyday experience that we take for granted, brush aside as disturbing or disruptive, attempt to understand, sometimes long for, often wrestle with and fear, and in the late twentieth century, try to "get in touch with." In the field of counselling and psychotherapy it is superfluous to suggest that emotion is central to the therapeutic process, because it is so very much at the core of human experience.

In life, individuals who show a general poverty of deep and lasting emotion and who cannot experience feelings of responsibility, remorse, shame, and gratitude are considered so abnormal that we recognize their deviance with a special diagnostic category: we say they have antisocial personality disorder and classify them as sociopaths. In fiction, those who are moved exclusively by reason are also viewed as aberrations, so different from ourselves that they capture our imagination. The very names of Conan Doyle's detective Sherlock Holmes and *Star Trek*'s Mr. Spock have become synonymous with superhuman rationality. Indeed, Mr. Spock is not a human being at all; he is an alien who visits among humans. Sherlock Holmes, relentless in his detachment, while able to feel is never duped by passion, and thus always remains principled and rational no matter what emotional temptations cross his path. Our lives, however, revolve around our feelings and those of others. Those of us who engage with our fellow humans as counsellors and therapists face this fact on a daily basis as part of our working life. As John Bowlby (1988) states:

> There are. . . no more important communications between one human being and another than those expressed emotionally, and no information more vital for constructing and reconstructing models of self and other than informa-

tion about how each feels toward the other. . . . Small wonder therefore, if. . . during the course of psychotherapy and restructuring of working models, it is the emotional communications between a patient and a therapist that play the crucial part. (pp. 156-157)

In this guidebook, I hope to accomplish two tasks. First, I will examine some common assumptions about emotion in order to arrive at a deeper understanding of current approaches to emotion, especially as these exist in the fields of psychology and counselling. Then I will offer a new framework for working with emotional experience. This I developed in part as a result of coming to terms with my clients' and my own frustrations and struggles with the dominant approaches to emotion, and in part through educating myself in the new ways of understanding emotion that are currently emerging.

Let us begin with the word emotion itself. Webster's (1988) dictionary offers the following definition:

Emotion: a strong feeling (such as fear, wonder, love, sorrow, shame) often accompanied by a physical reaction (e.g., blushing or trembling).

Emotion is so commonly described as *feeling*, both in dictionaries and in everyday usage, that we simply take for granted that by emotion we invariably mean feeling. I will not seek to dispute this assumption here. I do, however, note it. I note also that when we speak of emotion or feeling we also assume that it is mostly something physical:

Feeling: the act or state of someone who feels; the effect conveyed by the sense of touch; sensation in general; bodily power to feel. (Webster, 1988)

As well, feeling is described as noncognitive ("an intuitive belief, a conviction based on grounds other than reason"), where intuition is defined as a perception arrived at in the absence of conscious rational processes (Webster, 1988).

Embedded in such language is the notion that emotion and feeling are sensation-based bodily functions. These definitions reinforce the conception that emotion is feeling and that feeling (and therefore emotion) involves no process of discernment, evaluation, or judgment. Thus defined, both in formal and in everyday usage, emotion becomes a physiological, a bodily experience, not a cognitive one. This notion is even more noticeable when we examine definitions of thinking.

> Thinking: to engage in the process of arranging ideas in a pattern of relationships or of adding new ideas in a pattern of relationships or of adding new ideas soon to be related to a pattern; to turn things over in the mind, e.g., to consider advantages or disadvantages, . . . to have consideration or concern, . . . to make provision, . . . to conceive in the mind, . . . to work out by reasoning. (Webster, 1988)

Thinking as defined here is a voluntary act under the control and direction of the thinker, whereas emotion/feeling wells up through the senses in the body and does not involve choice. Thinking is seen as a mental activity based on reason, reflection, consideration, and choice, while emotion/feeling is a sense-based physiological and unbidden response.

In Western culture we have long been accustomed to separate mind from body and thinking from feeling. Mind and thought are rational; body and feeling are irrational. Reason is the noblest function among humans, the prime and possibly only legitimate means to gaining knowledge. Since Plato, we have energetically set about subjecting nature, society, and consciousness to reason. The rational has become synonymous with sense, the nonrational with non-sense. Feeling, because of its association with the nonrational, has been robbed of its sense-making possibilities. Thus in much of Western philosophical and scientific tradition, emotion has largely been viewed as disruptive to reason, and therefore a problem that must somehow be controlled.

This notion that the rational should rule the emotional, that the head should rule the heart, is termed "rational supremacy" by Michael Mahoney (1991). Rational supremacy is reflected in much of the literature about emotion in the fields of psychology and counselling.

Chapter 1 of this guidebook examines and disputes the historical basis for rational supremacy, and lays the groundwork for a more proactive approach to emotion. Each subsequent chapter develops the interconnecting aspects of a strategy for the positive use of emotional experience.

Emotion in Psychology: An Historical Overview

Psychology, and with it psychotherapy and counselling, emerged in the 1870s as a scientific field that defined itself as separate from philosophy and physiology. Since that time psychologists, like philosophers and physiologists before them, have concerned themselves with understanding and explaining emotion. Early psychological theories of emotion assumed conceptualizations of emotion that predated the new discipline, and therefore treated emotions as physiological events that could be explained in terms of bodily sensation.

Emotion as Neurophysiological Response

In the late nineteenth century both William James, an American psychologist, and James Lange, a Danish physiologist, working completely independently of each other, reached the same conclusion: sensation precedes emotion. That is, felt emotion is the feedback from neurological and physiological changes in the central nervous system and the brain that occurs in response to the situations we encounter. It is through our physiological responses that we recognize our emotional state. In other words, physiological changes are the antecedents of emotion.

In the years since the James-Lange theory (as it was called) was posited, Walter Cannon (1927) successfully argued that the theory cannot hold because (1) the same neurological and physiological changes can accompany very different emotional states; (2) changes to internal organs, which James and Lange saw as sources for emotional signals, occur too slowly to account for changes in emotion; (3) artificial induction of physiological changes does not produce particular emotions; and (4) the same physiological changes that accompany emotion can also be observed in states of disease such as fever, chills, and hypoglycemia, and these are not typically confused with emotion. Cannon did not seek to deny the presence of physiological changes in emotion; in fact, he believed that bodily changes and the experience of emotion occur at the same time. What he objected to was the claim that visceral and skeletal responses cause emotion. He and others (Bard, 1934; Schachter & Singer, 1962) were able to demonstrate that the physiological aspects of emotion do not occur as antecedents that determine emotional experience. Instead, they were able to show that while neurological and physiological arousal are definitely a part of emotional experience, emotion could neither be reduced to, nor explained only in terms of, arousal.

Emotion as Instinct and Psychic Energy

While James, Lange, Cannon, Bard, and others grappled with the idea of emotions as neurological and physiological events, Sigmund Freud formulated a theory of emotion based on a different premise. Like the aforementioned thinkers, Freud also conceived of emotion as body-based and somehow located in the central nervous system. But his explanation, rather than looking to neurophysiology, relied on the language of physics and mechanics. Freud described emotion in terms of psychic and libidinal (sexual and life) energies. For him, the emotions were quantities and forces tied to instinct, operating from the unconscious, contained inside us, and governed by the same physical principles that govern boilers and hydraulics systems. Accordingly, feelings were forces under pressure that arose outside the agency of the conscious and rational mind, acted independently of it, demanded discharge, and compelled us to behave in ways that had nothing whatever to do with rationality.

Freud, while positing a physics-based mechanistic theory of emotion, made no effort to operationalize his hypothesis and test his theory. He simply inferred it from his own observations and borrowed language from other disciplines to help him articulate his ideas. In many ways, Freud's theory can be thought of as a literary theory of emotion because he relied so heavily on metaphor to illustrate his point.

Emotion as Expression Caused by Antecedent Events

The theories described thus far hold in common that the body and the central nervous system are involved in emotional processes, and that conscious agency is not. As well, they all hold that emotion is caused (i.e., stimulated or called up) by the conditions or events, whether internal or external, that precede it.

Emotion is an effect, the cause of which is to be found elsewhere. Freud found the cause of emotion in the instincts and the unconscious, outside the rational mind. Behaviorists, while taking exception to Freud's explanations for cause, concurred with the idea that emotion was an other-than-rational process. Guided by assumptions that there is nothing innate about human behavior and that, therefore, everything we do and everything we are is learned through a process of conditioning, and committed to the notion that only objectively observable data are allowable for study, behaviorists viewed all psychological processes, including feeling, only in terms of their outwardly observable manifestations (behaviors) and explained them in terms of the stimuli (the antecedent events) that caused them. In that case, emotion could be explained only as a conditioned response and was nothing other than its expression in behavior. Feelings were reduced to and recognizable in characteristic behavioral patterns. For example, rage was the clenching of fists and teeth, the flushing of the skin, the dilation of the nostrils. Sadness was the bowing of the head, the turning down of the corners of the mouth, the tears flowing from the eyes. This understanding of emotion still persists and has prompted some provocative research findings.

Paul Ekman, a psychologist who has been studying emotion as expression for some twenty years, has been able to demonstrate that it is possible to modify one's emotional state through deliberately controlling the voluntary musculature of the face and body. He has shown that even when one feels sad, if one intentionally draws out the lips and turns up the corners of the mouth in the form of a smile (behaviors usually associated with feeling happy), visceral events that are associated with happiness begin to occur, and at the same time, one's emotional state changes from sadness to happiness. Ekman has trained himself to control all the muscles in his face and is able to produce, at will, facial expressions that he has investigated cross-culturally and found to be consistently associated with given emotions. As he produces these expressions, he is also able to produce the emotion that generally occurs in tandem with the expression he is purposefully creating.

With training from Ekman, others have also been able to learn this skill. While demonstrating that expression (i.e., behavior) affects physiology (visceral response), Ekman has also demonstrated that intention (what one chooses to do) plays a big part in feeling. If it is possible to initiate feelings by choice, and to affect emotion with conscious manipulation of facial expression, gesture, and posture, then feeling and emotion can no longer be conceived as only physiologically and neurologically based, involuntary reactions and responses to antecedent events. Intention and choice can play a major role in emotional experience. What, then, accounts for intention and choice?

Cognitive behaviorists, who in the 1950s began to distinguish themselves from more traditional behaviorists by allowing for the effects of internalized learning and conditioning (e.g., thinking) upon behavior, were willing to link cognition with emotion. Believing that thinking could have an effect upon behavior, they suggested that thoughts could be antecedent events that cause feeling and that, therefore, a change in thinking could cause a change in feeling. Feeling, however, always followed thought; it never preceded it. It therefore remained an outcome, an effect dependent upon the antecedent event (the thought) that caused it. Cognitive behaviorists' acceptance of the possibility that internal conscious processes could affect behavior signalled a significant shift in focus for behaviorists and did at least link cognition with emotion. But it did not change the common understanding of emotion as an involuntary response dependent on the stimuli that caused it.

Ekman's findings, however, do suggest that one can actually choose and produce emotions, or voluntarily alter the feelings that one is experiencing. That means we can initiate our feelings of our own accord. This raises the question: What is at work in the making of such a choice? Cognitive behaviorists seek to answer that question with the suggestion that it is thought which drives the emotional process — i.e., I think in certain ways about my experiences, and my thinking therefore causes my emotional experience. Other theorists disagree. For them, this conception of the process is a form of rational supremacy. They argue that emotion is a complex, nonlinear process that can be understood as a constitutive (i.e., a constructive and formative) activity, rather than only as a reactive response.

Emotion as Constitutive of Experience

The antithesis to both rational supremacy and the reduction of emotion to reactive bodily function emerges from a combination of theories. Robert Solomon (1983), a philosopher at the University of Texas at Austin, states his premise this way:

> Our passions have too long been relegated to mere footnotes in philosophy and parentheses in psychology, as if they were intrusions and interruptions — sometimes welcome distractions but more usually embarrassing if not treacherous subversions of lives that ought to be conceived in "higher" terms.
>
> Our passions constitute our lives.
>
> It is our passions, and our passions alone, that provide our lives with meaning. (p. xvi)

Instead of treating feelings as if they were primitive, instinctual reactions that overwhelm us from within and require the cool and controlling hand of reason, Solomon moves feeling into the center of our existence. According to him, our emotions are not disturbances or intrusions at all. He believes that feeling, rather than distracting us from experience, actually grounds us in it by giving experience meaning and value. Feelings are not merely impulses, they are

> ... *judgments* with which we structure the world to our purposes, carve out a universe in our own terms, measure the facts of reality, and ultimately "constitute" not only our world but ourselves. Rather than disturbances or intrusions, these emotions, and the passions in general, are the very core of our existence, the system of meanings and values within which our lives either develop and grow or starve and stagnate. The passions are the very soul of our existence; it is not they that require the controls and rationalizations of reason. Rather, it is reason that requires the anchorage and earthy wisdom of the passions. (Solomon, 1983, p. xix)

In placing feeling at the center of human experience, Solomon takes an approach similar to that taken by the so-called third force or humanist orientation toward emotion. Humanist psychology, which includes existential, person-centered and Gestalt therapy, developed out of a reaction to the two other major theoretical approaches (psychoanalysis and behaviorism). Theorists from the third force objected to the psychoanalytic position that freedom is restricted by unconscious forces, irrational drives, and past events. They also objected to the behaviorist position that all behavior is determined and restricted by sociocultural conditioning. Instead, humanists believe that while we may be limited in our choices by circumstance, we are nonetheless free to inform ourselves of the meaning of our actions and to choose our own reactions and responses to those circumstances (Corey, 1991, p. 174). For humanists, the meaning and particularly the value of our experience arise out of our feelings. Like Robert Solomon, humanist thinkers and therapists place feeling at the center of human experience as the function that guides sensing, acting, and reflecting, and thus "fuels both action and awareness" (Mahoney, 1991, p. 206).

Feelings are not merely the "expressions of the 'spillover' of excessive psychic energy, which often take the form of neurotic symptoms, denied impulses and defense mechanisms" (Mahoney, 1991, p. 205), as psychoanalysts would describe them. Neither are feelings simply "conditioned responses that can themselves serve as discriminative stimuli for other responses [which] often have an undesirable disorganizing effect on skilled behavior" (Mahoney, 1991, p. 205), as behaviorists would have them. Nor are they "the products of thoughts and images" (Mahoney, 1991, p. 206), the aftermath of cognitive processes, that cognitive behaviorists seek to control with thought. For humanists, and in some ways for Solomon, feelings are the "prime movers in the interaction of thought and emotion" (Mahoney, 1991, p. 190). Solomon goes a little further. He considers the emotions "our own doings. . . . Emotions are not dumb forces beyond our control but judgments we make. As such, they have conceptual and intelligent form. . ." (Solomon, 1983, p. 251). In conceiving of feeling in this way, Solomon aligns himself with an approach to philosophy and psychology that emphasizes the active participation in perception of the person undergoing the experience.

This approach has a long and honorable history dating back to Giambattista Vico, founder of the philosophy of history, who also gave us the first recorded and organized presentation of the roles played by perception, imagination, and previous knowledge in the organization of experience. He asserted that humans create order in their experience by superimposing the familiar onto the unfamiliar. Stating that "to know " is "to make," Vico anticipated by more than two hundred years the Swiss psychologist Jean Piaget's declaration that to know an object is to act upon it (Mahoney, 1991, p. 98). After Vico, the genealogy of this understanding of the process of perception reaches to Immanuel Kant who suggested that the mind, rather than being a blank slate upon which experience inscribes the sum total of all knowledge, is actually "an active organ which molds and coordinates sensation into ideas, . . . [and] transforms the chaotic multiplicity of experience into the ordered unity of thought" (Durant, 1926, p. 291). From Kant the lineage can be traced to Hans Vaihinger, the Kantian scholar who argued that psychological processes are not merely passive internal receptors that reflect external reality, much as mirrors reflect the objects placed in front of them. Rather, he believed, as did Kant, that these processes have an instrumental and functional significance for human action and survival:

> . . . The psyche is an organic formative force which independently changes what has been appropriated, and can adapt foreign elements to its own requirements as easily as it adapts itself to what is new. The mind is not merely appropriative, it is also assimilative and constructive. (Vaihinger, 1924 [1911], p. 2)

Vaihinger influenced Alfred Adler who, after breaking with Freud and his notions of biological determinism in 1911, founded a new psychology based on the notion that human behavior is purposeful and directed and not merely the outcome of heredity and environment. Adler's influence stretches to the present through the work of Rudolph Dreikurs and is strongly felt in the field of education. Other well-known Freudian revisionists like Harry Stack Sullivan, Karen Horney, and Eric Fromm also adopted the Adlerian notion that behavior can be most readily understood in terms of the ways in which we as individuals actively organize our perceptions of our lifeworlds (Corey, 1991, pp. 137-138).

Perception as Organizing Activity

Carl Jung, perhaps the most famous of those psychologists who broke with Freud, recognized early the effect of the processes of perception upon human behavior. For him perception was a complex process of mentation involving the four psychological functions of sensing, thinking, feeling, and intuiting, which he regarded as equal in importance and validity in their contribution to the human process of forming knowledge and understanding. Jung, like the aforementioned thinkers, believed that the structuring of experience is an active process involving the participation of the individual, who is more than a mere recipient of information from the external world. Jean Piaget expressed it this way: "Intelligence organizes its world by organizing itself" (cited in von Glaserfeld, 1984, p. 24). Michael Mahoney (1991) describes this kind of organizational activity as "proactive cognition and participatory knowing," summarizing it as follows:

> . . . All cognitive phenomena — from perception and memory to problem solving and consciousness — entail active and proactive processes. In less technical terms, the organism is an active participant in its own experience as well as in learning. We are, to repeat a theme, co-constructors of the personal realities to and from which we respond. Rather than just being a passive repository of sensory experience or a mechanical way station for information processing, the organism is portrayed as an active, anticipatory "embodied theory". (p. 100)

HEY WAITRESS! WHERE THE HELL ARE MY PANCAKES?!?

For these thinkers, the emotions are part of that "active, anticipatory 'embodied theory'." They are "powerful knowing processes that reflect individual patterns of organization and disorganization in experience" (Mahoney, 1991, p. 207). When conceived of in this way, feeling becomes an integral part of the process of creating judgments, evaluations, and interpretations. If we treat feeling as Jung does, as part of apperception — the process of understanding something perceived in terms of previous experience — we open up very different ways of dealing with feeling in the counselling process.

When feelings are seen as involuntary reactive and disruptive processes or as maladaptive patterns of behavior, as is the case in most therapeutic practices, they are generally treated as management problems. That means feelings are conceived of as potentially problematic reactions which require control. Whether the preferred intervention is expression and discharge so that catharsis and insight can take place, or reconditioning so that undesirable patterns of emotional reaction can be replaced, the goal of therapy is to manage and control feeling. The objective is to bring intensity of feeling to an acceptable level, or to eliminate those feelings that have been deemed negative or debilitative. From this perspective, the underlying message about emotion is that there is something wrong with strong feelings and that some feelings, especially those that don't make us happy, are bad. Such an approach can, according to my own findings and those of Mahoney, "actually impede a client's progress in integrating emotional experiences with changing patterns of activity and self-construal" (1991, p. 207).

In contrast to therapeutic interventions that seek to manage, control, or eliminate feeling, the approach favored here is to understand feelings and emotions as powerful ways of knowing. R. Vance Peavy (1992) articulates this position:

As a counsellor I recognize emotions and feelings to be powerful ways of knowing. . . . Emotions actually help us notice things and focus our attention. Emotions also warn us when our life or consciousness is too filled with disorder or chaos and is in danger of being overwhelmed. Feelings are important constituents of our relationships with others and even with objects and activities in our world. . . . Cultures vary in the amount of passion which characterizes customs, daily activities and everyday relationships. Even emotional expressions such as anger, sadness, resentment and fear are not in themselves phenomena in need of control — rather, they inform us that certain aspects of our lives are out of balance, neglected or in danger. As a counsellor, I try to help my clients use [the] felt knowledge [that feeling is] as a way of understanding. . . .

From this point of view, it is imperative not to treat the emotions as phenomena or events that require suppression, management, control, or cure. Rather, they are to be treated as helpful and informative sources of knowledge and understanding that are an integral and active part of our sense-making processes.

Feeling As a Way of Knowing

What Are Ways of Knowing?

Ways of knowing are the active and reflective processes that we use to structure and organize our experience in the course of forming knowledge and understanding. In his description of the human psyche, Carl Jung (1928) recognized four distinct psychic functions or ways of knowing oneself and the world. He suggested that as human beings, we know through sensing, thinking, feeling, and intuiting, and that each of these functions or ways of knowing has an important, equally valid contribution to make. Therefore, no one function or way of knowing has greater value or importance, nor can any be singled out as the ultimate or necessary one to be developed as an organizer for the rest. The four psychic functions, or ways of knowing, are described below.

Sensing

Sensing involves the discovery of the order and structure in experience.

> Sensing is perception by means of the senses. It is one of the two cognitive perceptual functions that receive information. Sensing is the immediate recording of sights, sounds, smells, tastes, and touch impressions. . . . The sensing function is a realistic, empirical function concerned with actualities. (Singer & Loomis, 1984, p. 15)

When we use the sensing function, we tend to interact with what actually happens or exists without deciding whether it is right or wrong. That is, we discriminate without judging; we differentiate without ranking. When using the sensing function, we notice details and describe differences impartially.

The sensing function in action directs and informs us. It tells us this is red and that is blue; turn right here, don't turn left; this is sweet, that is savory. It focuses upon the distinctions and dimensions that contribute to making things particular. For example, when we are eating an ice cream cone, the sensing function registers the taste (vanilla honey), the temperature (cold), the texture (smooth for the ice cream, rough for the cone, sticky for the melted bits that have run down the edge). Sensing deals with a fact-based understanding of what is there; it does not concern itself with further dimensions of the experience.

Intuiting

Intuiting involves the grasping of possibility in experience. Intuition is

. . . perception via unconscious processes. Intuition integrates information received subliminally, either from the physical world or from the inner subjective realm. This information emerges full-blown as a complete idea or vision of the potential in things. (Singer & Loomis, 1984, p. 17)

Intuition is not bound by reason or logic and is responsible for creative leaps that may move knowledge forward to new paradigms. The intuitive function is perpetually "brainstorming" and reworking existing conditions. It thrives on change.

The intuitive function sees potential and suggests alternatives. For example, when we are eating an ice cream cone, intuition remarks that we might remove the ice cream from the cone and place it in a dish, surround it with strawberries and pour hot chocolate sauce over it; that instead of a cone, we might have a sundae, or even a banana split. Intuition does not concern itself so much with what it finds directly as with what it might create out of what it finds.

Thinking

Thinking involves the discovery of theoretical and practical logic and reason in experience.

Thinking is the processing function that reaches decisions through logical step-by-step deliberations. It weighs pros and cons and rationally determines outcomes. As the problem-solving function, thinking is concerned with cause-and-effect relationships. (Singer & Loomis, 1984, p. 13)

Thinking proceeds along a course of impersonal, reasoned reflection and is aimed at systematically producing theories that explain the whys and wherefores of experience.

The thinking function concerns itself with how things fit together and what makes them work. For example, when we are eating an ice cream cone, the thinking function asks the questions: What ingredients are in this product? Is the flavor natural or artificial? Are the strawberries fresh? How much sugar is in this product? Is it reasonable for me to eat this ice cream now, or should I wait until I've had my dinner? How will eating this ice cream affect my diet?

Thinking concerns itself with a reason-based analysis of experience.

Feeling

Feeling involves the discovery of personal and relational values in experience. Feeling arranges the world and everything in it according to evaluations based on acceptance or rejection. Feeling works along such value dimensions as like/dislike, agreeable/disagreeable, pleasant/unpleasant. Such evaluations may include emotional components (e.g., love, hate, jealousy, rage), but it would be incorrect to define value judgments solely as emotions. These value dimensions align with our personal and sociocultural value systems. The degree to which we either share our values with others, or are able to join empathically in understanding the experiences of others from their point of view, is affected by our ability to use our feeling function.

Feeling focuses on what matters most in the moment. For example, when we are eating an ice cream cone, the feeling function appreciates the flavor and decides this ice cream tastes good. It evaluates the choice to eat an ice cream before dinner as acceptable, and appreciates the aesthetic of transforming the ice cream cone into a sundae. While thinking may weigh the consequences of ice cream in relation to our diet, feeling decides that today we prefer the ice cream despite the calories. It may wrestle with thought later on, and under the influence of thought, may reverse priorities and judge the act of eating the ice cream as ultimately wrong. This judgment could manifest through guilt, anxiety, or some other emotion that communicates the meaning of the experience. Feeling values the experience, and the emotional name we give our feeling captures and communicates the meanings we have ascribed.

CARL JUNG IN A BAR-FIGHT

Feeling has so often been construed as synonymous with emotion that we should distinguish between the two before attempting to discuss the interactions among the four ways of knowing.

Feeling and Emotion Distinguished

The notion that feeling is a function that judges and orders reality according to values is the basis for working constructively with emotion. Up to this point, we have noted but not questioned the common practice of using the terms feeling and emotion as if they were synonymous. However, if we are to understand feeling as a way of knowing, we must now distinguish between feeling and emotion.

Feeling is the way of knowing that we use to discern and judge how and what we value. When we are feeling, we are deciding in a very basic and fundamental way whether we accept or reject whatever is occurring now. Feeling is an active process of choosing for or against. When we are feeling, we are actively engaged. We are loving or hating, liking or disliking, wanting more or wanting less, moving toward or moving away. We know we are working with feeling as a way of knowing when we are using evaluative verbs such as these.

Feeling is the making of value judgments; emotion is the outcome of that evaluation. Emotions are the adjectival labels we apply to our experience once feeling choices have been made. For example, if I choose to like something, I might say, "That's great!" I have made my choice, and then assigned to it words that express my evaluation. The emotions that we recognize, name, and apply to our experience as a result of how we value it, inform us about the feeling judgments we have made. Feeling orients us in relation to that which we experience. Feeling tells us whether we are attracted or repelled by the things we are experiencing. The emotional names or evaluative adjectives that we attach to our feelings help us bring to awareness what we have decided. The emotions that we use to describe our feelings communicate the quality, kind, and degree of judgment for or against that we have made of our experience. Therefore, when we use feeling as a way of knowing, we are using this function in the same way we might use a compass. Feeling can be thought of as a tool that helps to situate us in experience relative to our values. We then use the language of emotion to help us illustrate, describe, and articulate our values.

The naming of experience with the language of emotion helps us to capture our experience with words so that we can understand and communicate it both to ourselves and to others. For example, as I eat my ice cream, I may tell myself that I feel content. In doing so, I have summarized a whole host of judgments in one small word. I am saying that I value positively my choice and my experience of eating the ice cream, that I like what I am doing and derive satisfaction and comfort from it. I am also saying that I am not in conflict with myself over the choice that I have made, and that it is congruent with my personal values. I may also be saying that I appreciate myself for making this choice and the conditions of my life for making it possible for me to eat ice cream and not regret it later. My choice of descriptors is an indication of my whole appraisal of my experience with ice cream. This holds true for all the words we use to describe our emotional experience.

The possibilities and implications encapsulated in the language of emotion will be further explored in Chapter 3. There we will also look into the world of meaning that emotion-words offer us. We will investigate the use of a vocabulary of emotion, how this vocabulary offers us entry points into feeling as a way of knowing, and how emotional experience can be a resource for understanding ourselves and others.

However, before we go more deeply into these topics, we must acknowledge that feeling as a way of knowing is not everyone's strong suit. Therefore, we must first explore how feeling as a way of knowing can interact with the other three functions, and how individual preferences for the various ways of knowing can affect our use of feeling and emotion as a resource.

Interactive Dimensions of the Psychological Functions

The four functions of sensing, intuiting, thinking, and feeling can be described separately but are always interacting with each other. All human beings use all four functions all the time. But individuals tend to develop them to different degrees and to rely upon some more than others. Our preferences in using the four functions depend both on personal inclinations and on influences exerted upon us by the sociocultural and contextual conditions in which we find ourselves.

Understanding these individual preferences and priorities in ways of knowing is extremely useful, especially when dealing with emotional experience, as one invariably does in counselling. Therefore, even if our priority is working with feeling and emotion, it is useful to investigate to what degree a client has developed the feeling function in relation to the other functions. This will help to situate that individual with regard to his or her unique way of dealing with the world.

Recognizing preferences in ways of knowing helps the counsellor both to comprehend and to enter into a client's emotional experience in a way that will be respectful and meaningful to that individual's unique way of dealing with the world. To facilitate this understanding, the "Ways of Knowing" Profile — a simple diagnostic tool — is included on pages 26 - 29.

Use of the Diagnostic Tool

The "Ways of Knowing" Profile can be used to create and develop an understanding of how an individual engages in the process of structuring and organizing experience. The numerical values indicate primarily which ways of knowing are favored over others, the order of their relative importance, the conditions that must be satisfied in order for an individual to proceed, and the degree to which that individual has developed each function relative to the others. This tool is not a test of type or personality. It does provide a map of the pathway an individual may follow, under most conditions, in the process of making sense of experience. The scores obtained for each function or way of knowing should not be treated as discrete units of measurement. They are simply indicators of the relative degree to which an individual relies upon particular ways of knowing in relation to the other possible ways.

If all the scores are relatively close together (e.g., sensing =26, thinking =27, feeling =24, intuiting =23), the individual will still have preferences in the process of organizing experience, but will have relatively easy access to all four ways of knowing. If, however, the scores show greater variation (e.g., sensing =34, thinking =29, feeling =19, intuiting =18), clear preferences and degrees of use and development are indicated, and some ways of knowing (in this case, sensing and thinking) are much more heavily relied upon and play a much greater role in the process of structuring and organizing experience. Having this information helps both client and counsellor to form an understanding of the client's experience.

"Ways of Knowing" Profile

On the scoring sheet, please rank each of the four statements in each of the 10 questions in order of their importance to you (4, 3, 2, 1), so that 4 most closely describes you and 1 least describes you. You may find it difficult to choose between some of the statements in some of questions, and may wish to assign the same value to two or more statements — but this is not an option. In each of the 10 questions, only one statement may receive the value 4, 3, 2, or 1.

1. My approach to forming knowledge and understanding is
    a. _____ based on looking at the facts
    b. _____ based on logic and reason
    c. _____ based on my feelings and emotions
    d. _____ based on my immediate intuitive reaction or response

2. I would describe myself as
    a. _____ concerned with accuracy, with getting things right
    b. _____ interested in investigating and learning more about the things I come across
    c. _____ liking things that can be dramatized or vividly pictured
    d. _____ liking to jump into things and/or take some risks

3. Information is most likely to catch my attention if it is

    a. _____ reliable, stable, and properly standardized

    b. _____ known for its proven excellence because it has been thoroughly researched

    c. _____ creatively and attractively presented

    d. _____ able to help me gain a deeper personal understanding

4. My approach to learning is

    a. _____ learning by doing

    b. _____ learning by thinking things through

    c. _____ learning by getting involved with others

    d. _____ learning through sudden insight, through having "ah-ha" experiences

5. I like to

    a. _____ be careful with details and keep things in order

    b. _____ think about all kinds of ideas and theories

    c. _____ be conscious of and sensitive to what is going on with the people around me

    d. _____ use my imagination to come up with new ways of doing things

6. In my approach to accomplishing a task I am

    a. _____ careful about details, and make sure that I do everything that is required

    b. _____ reasonable, and think about how best to work my way toward my goal

    c. _____ guided by how I feel about the task, and have to feel like doing it

    d. _____ challenged and engaged if the task requires me to find solutions to problems

7. In general, I would describe myself as
   - a. _____ concrete and practical
   - b. _____ inquiring and comparative
   - c. _____ responsive and able to put myself in other people's shoes
   - d. _____ able to create new ideas and experiences out of what is offered

8. When I work with documented materials, I look for
   - a. _____ a clear, concise arrangement of information
   - b. _____ evidence to show that the information provided is accurate and well-researched
   - c. _____ a tasteful composition and a pleasing synthesis of knowledge
   - d. _____ material that suggests several different ways of approaching the subject matter

9. I like to
   - a. _____ stick with things, and follow through until all is properly completed
   - b. _____ analyze things into their component parts so that I can understand how they all work together
   - c. _____ respond to beauty and do artistic things
   - d. _____ try different things in different situations, play with things to see how they work

10. Mostly, I like to
   - a. _____ deal with concrete things in a hands-on fashion and know what outcomes will be produced
   - b. _____ check things out to make sure that they are correct, proven, reasonable, and true
   - c. _____ deal with people rather than things
   - d. _____ be inventive and come up with new and different approaches

How to Score Your "Ways of Knowing" Profile

1. Add all the values you placed in the "a" section of each question. Transfer this total to the category entitled Sensing in the space provided below.

2. Add all the values you placed in the "b" section of each question. Transfer this total to the category entitled Thinking in the space provided below.

3. Add all the values you placed in the "c" section of each question. Transfer this total to the category entitled Feeling in the space provided below.

4. Add all the values you placed in the "d" section of each question. Transfer this total to the category entitled Intuiting in the space provided below.

The overall total of your scores taken together must equal 100. If that is not the case, it is likely that you have made an error in addition, or have inadvertently given the same value to two statements on one of the questions.

These totals taken in order of highest to lowest constitute your personal "Ways of Knowing" Profile.

Scoring

a. _____ Sensing

b. _____ Thinking

c. _____ Feeling

d. _____ Intuiting

Five Case Studies

The following five case studies illustrate how the "Ways of Knowing" Profile can be used as an interpretive tool, and why it is important for the counsellor to keep the client's profile in mind.

Client 1

Profile Scores:

Sensing, 22; Thinking, 21; Feeling, 25; Intuiting, 32.

Pathway Through Experience

Starting Point: Intuiting

This client relies upon intuition as her perceptual way of knowing and making sense. Her intuitive grasp of her experience determines how she organizes it and how she will proceed. She is usually immediately conscious of the meanings and possibilities inherent in a given situation. Her perceptions crystallize via the unconscious and rise to awareness either as an insight, a creative innovation, or a synchronistic understanding of present conditions as linked to previous experience. The potential in a situation and its inherent possibilities are foremost in her mind. She organizes her responses to events and structures her decisions in relation to these perceived meanings and possibilities. This suggests that she acts out of her own keenly felt subjective experience first, then organizes her feeling, thinking, and acting accordingly.

The Knowing Process

Having formed an intuitive understanding of a given situation or condition, this client then processes her experience by judging it according to her personal values. She decides whether it is good or bad, pleasant or unpleasant, valuable, desirable, useful or not. She also places the experience in a relational context in that she will engage empathically and sympathetically with any others who may also be involved. Her feelings are consciously available to her and enter into her assessment of her situation. At the same time, she includes sensing in her judgment forming process. As she evaluates her experience through feeling as the way of knowing that guides her judgments, she is conscious of her sense impressions, notices details, and is able to incorporate and order this information. As she forms her judgments, she also deliberates upon them. Although feeling comes first, the small numerical differences between feeling, sensing, and thinking indicate that once an intuitive grasp has been reached, the other functions can act in concert and are included nearly equally in the sense-making process.

Because this client relies upon intuiting as a way of knowing to a greater degree than the other functions available to her, it is likely that she may be at a loss for action if she finds herself in conditions that she cannot immediately grasp intuitively. It could be argued that although she has developed the other three functions nearly equally, these are somewhat dependent on her intuition, which provides the raw material out of which she constructs her other responses. Knowing proceeds smoothly for her when her intuition can readily engage with her experience.

If that is not the case, as it might not be in circumstances when one of the other three ways of knowing dominates — e.g., the demand is made that she begin with logical analysis, or describe sensation first, or she is asked to say what she feels before she has had the opportunity to structure her understanding through interpretation, or her intuitive interpretation is negated — she may be at a loss for answers or may become inarticulate about her experience. At that point, feeling as a way of knowing may alert her to her discomfort in that she will be aware of her own unwillingness to proceed. Sensing, especially internal sensing (bodily feedback from the autonomic nervous system), may send out warning signals. Thinking, the creation of a logical analysis of a given situation, will prove awkward.

This client's preparatory grasp of what is to be understood is intuitive. Whether her intuitions are correct or not is not as important to her process of knowing as the articulation of the potentials and possibilities that she perceives. Since interpretation and reinterpretation are constant with this individual, she can make changes, modifications, and re-evaluations as she moves through her process. The counsellor who works with her must not stifle her perceptions. Once the client has articulated and explored these, she will not necessarily retain them. If, however, the counsellor denies the client's perceptions or dismisses them out of hand, the client may become entrenched or defensive (perhaps aggressively so) and in the last analysis, may withdraw. Her feeling function will then evaluate her circumstances as disagreeable, and the emotional names she will use to capture her experience will reflect this. She may also begin to use ways of knowing that, for her, are less sophisticated. For example, she may use thinking to rationalize her behavior with faulty logic, or require a slowing down of her process so that she can build a basic picture with sensing in a concrete, step-by-step, information-based way, one piece at a time. It may appear as if she has become unable to grasp what is required.

She will be best able to access other ways of knowing if she is invited to speak about her overall intuitive grasp first. Asking her questions about how she understands things and what they mean to her will generally make it possible for her to say both what she feels and thinks and to give a sense-based description of her experience. Once she has articulated her intuitive grasp, the other ways of knowing will come into play and work harmoniously to round out or alter her understanding.

Client 2

Profile Scores:

Sensing, 22; Thinking, 24; Feeling, 20; Intuiting, 34.

Pathway Through Experience

Starting Point: Intuiting

This client begins his sense-making process much in the same way as Client 1. Again, potential and possibility are of primary importance, and knowing is experienced as insight, creative understanding, and the convergence of multiple perspectives or options. As with Client 1, other ways of knowing operate in relation to this intuitive starting point.

The Knowing Process

Having formed an intuitive understanding of a given situation, this client then moves to the thinking function. This usually means entering into a long process of deliberation that involves gathering detailed data, analyzing cause-effect relationships, and systematically categorizing information hierarchically. He spends time uncovering the logic of his situation, and as he proceeds, he also begins to use the sensing function. He impartially notices sense-based details, which he catalogues and records, and uses these to discover and create order. Only after he has engaged in this process of moving back and forth, altering his primary intuitive grasp in the light of more detailed information, will he engage the feeling function and judge his task, activity, or experience according to his values. It is unlikely that he will form feeling judgments until he has spent some time creating logical order out of his experience. It will not be practical or workable to ask him to use his feeling function as a way of knowing and making sense of experience before he has arrived at a structured understanding of what he encounters.

Like Client 1, this individual relies upon intuition as a way of knowing to a greater degree than he relies upon the other three functions. Also like Client 1, he will be at a loss for action if he finds himself in conditions that he cannot immediately intuitively grasp, or if he is asked to begin his process of knowing from a different standpoint. Although thinking, sensing, and feeling are developed almost to the same degree (their numerical scores are not substantially different), the intuition score, by comparison, is ten points higher than thinking, twelve points higher than sensing, and fourteen points higher than feeling. This indicates that intuiting is the way of knowing most easily accessible to this client and the one most readily relied upon. Although we are all capable of using all the ways of knowing available to us, we have clear preferences for the order in which we engage in them, and we tend to slow down or stop our process if conditions do not allow us to participate through those ways of knowing with which we are most familiar.

Accordingly, we can assume that the counsellor working with this client would have difficulty proceeding with communicating and forming understanding if she were to ask him to elaborate on feeling first, before inviting him to articulate his intuitive grasp, followed by his logical analysis, and his data-based summation of his experience. Even if the counsellor's primary intention is to help the client with feeling as a way of knowing, she must first understand how he relates to feeling before asking him to engage in feeling work. By comparison, Client 1 is much closer to feeling as a way of knowing than Client 2. Client 1 requires fewer intervening steps before she activates feeling. Nevertheless, the counsellor still must make room for Client 1's intuition first; otherwise, she will dance around a description of feeling until she has an intuitive organization of her experience from which to work. Client 2 requires more time and information before he can be asked to work with his feelings. He will also require a reasonable and logical justification for why feeling should be brought into the construction of his understandings. For feeling to be a part of his process, it must first "fit" with his intuition, and then make sense.

Successful feeling work depends upon the counsellor's finely tuned respect for the client's unique integration of ways of knowing. In the counselling process, premature demands for feeling can backfire.

Client 3

Profile Scores:

Sensing, 31; Thinking, 27; Feeling, 19; Intuiting, 23.

Pathway Through Experience

Starting Point: Sensing

This client relies upon sensing as the perceptual way of knowing through which he structures his process of forming understanding. He approaches his experience through the immediate recording of sights, sounds, smells, tastes, touch impressions, and through other bodily sensations. He is concerned first of all with actualities, with details, and with order. He proceeds by building a step-by-step, chronologically structured, concrete and functionally grounded model of what he finds and what is expected of him. The structure and order of existing conditions and the rules and standards of how things work are foremost in his mind.

The Knowing Process

Having outlined the sense-based details and the order present in the experience in question, this client then looks for reasoned and rationally based explanations. Like Client 2, he will spend time uncovering the logic of his situation. If he can uncover some logic in his experience, he will then consider the possibilities inherent in what he has uncovered. Only after having structured, analyzed, examined, and expanded upon his experience will he assess it with the feeling function. As with Client 2, feeling does not come into play until the other functions have done their work. Feeling as a way of knowing is not easily accessible to this client, and he may find it difficult to articulate what he feels. His profile scores (thinking, 27; feeling, 19) show that thinking and feeling do not act in conjunction with each other to the degree that they do with Client 1, or with individuals who have scores that are closer

together for these two functions. This indicates that with regard to judgment formation, he relies much more on the analytic process, preferring logic to empathy as the direction-finder through which he orients his choices and declares his values. This does not mean that this individual has no feelings, or that he cannot understand feeling. It does mean that for him, feeling comes after he has engaged in his experience through the processes primarily of sensing and thinking, followed by intuiting or imagining. It may also mean that because sensing is so highly developed in relation to feeling, he may confuse his sense experiences, which will be strong and immediately accessible to him, with feeling. He may believe that sensation is feeling, and may need help in distinguishing between the two. For him, anger may indeed be the immediate visceral sensations that he experiences, rather than a manifestation of a finely tuned value judgment he has made. Unlike Client 1, who uses feeling as a way of organizing judgment, this individual, like Client 2, feels as a reaction to experience, which he first organizes by sensing and thinking. The counsellor who works with this client must pay time and attention to his sensing and thinking functions before introducing feeling work.

Client 4

Profile Scores:

Sensing, 28; Thinking, 17; Feeling, 30; Intuiting, 25.

Pathway Through Experience

Starting Point: Feeling/Sensing

This client begins her process by immediately knowing how she feels in a given situation. As she enters into the experience, she is keenly aware of and guided by her values and preferences, which act as direction-finders. Any individual who enters into a situation with feelings first, attunes very quickly to the mood, tone, and emotion present in that situation, as well as in herself. This does not necessarily mean that she will always have ready an articulate explanation of her values; it simply means that she will know how she is being affected (positively or negatively) by what she is experiencing. As indicated by her profile scores (feeling, 30; sensing, 28; intuiting, 25; thinking, 17), for this client, feeling is the way of knowing that is most present. But because feeling is only two steps away from sensing, the physical ordering and structuring part of knowing enters into the process almost at the same time as the evaluative part of knowing. This means that for this client, experience is strongly felt in the body because feeling and sensation reach awareness almost at the same time. Her preferences are immediately clear to her, and her convictions are strongly held. She filters her experience through her emotions, but as she does this, she also takes a practical, data-based and factual, even matter-of-fact approach to organizing and structuring that experience. She will experience a need for relatedness and a need for control at the same time. At times she may experience an internal conflict between her almost automatic move to judge a situation based on feeling and her nearly equally strong predilection to move through a situation in a fact-based, empirical, and detail-oriented manner, which requires reserving judgment until later. She will want to be understanding and empathic, and will find it relatively easy to put herself in another person's shoes; but at the same time, she will be ready to take charge of a situation and will want things to be done accurately and correctly. She may find herself justifying her feelings with facts. Her preferences, and her feelings and emotions, will be deeply rooted and not easily swayed.

The Knowing Process

In orienting herself through the feeling function, this client is guided in her decision and judgment process primarily by her internalized values and by relational considerations. These considerations will be tempered by an almost equal need for structure and order arising from sensing as a way of knowing. Therefore, while this client has the capacity to engage sensitively and relationally with others, she is also practical and task-oriented in her approach. When both the feeling and organizational needs have been met, she will then concern herself with the possibilities and meanings that are present in her situation. She will bring in-tuiting as a way of knowing into play, using insight and innovation as a way of expanding upon her experience. Quite of-ten, having brought feeling, sensing, and intuiting into play, this individual will have engaged in her experience to a degree that satisfies her, and will not necessarily concern herself with the kind of logical analysis that would spring from thinking as a way of knowing. As feeling offers a kind of logic that is consistent with each person's values and beliefs, sensing creates a certain order, and intuiting suggests further courses of action, the logic that arises from abstract reasoning or thinking may seem superfluous to this client. For her, cognition is a quick, strongly felt process; the thinking function seems to slow it down. To her, deliberating, sift-ing and sorting, and categorizing for theory's sake can seem like a waste of time. To demand this of her would be to invite her to experience frustration.

For the counsellor who works with this client, gaining access to feeling will not present a problem. It may, however, be diffi-cult for this client to think in terms of any other kind of logic but that which arises out of feeling and a sense-based structure. For her what is, is; and it is so almost immediately. While she is very capable of empathy, this client is also capable of believing that what she feels is also what others feel. In other words, because she feels strongly and is receptive and sensitive to feeling and emotion, she may confuse her feelings and emotions with those of others, and may need to take the time to consider that her per-ceptions, though valid for her, may not be applicable to others no matter how strongly she feels them. As well, because she is so able to know through feeling, she may be vulnerable to taking responsibility for the emotional experience of others. A balance between feeling and thinking would afford her a more differenti-ated understanding of the self and other, and such development is missing in her to some degree. The counsellor must therefore carefully and slowly introduce her to other possibilities for differ-ent kinds of logic and ways of knowing.

Client 5

Profile Scores:

Sensing, 27; Thinking, 31; Feeling, 15; Intuiting, 25.

Pathway Through Experience

Starting Point: Thinking

This client begins his process by slowly and carefully gathering together all relevant details and materials in order to analyze his situation. Foremost in his mind is a desire for information that is accurate and supported, because for him, action depends upon reflection, deliberation, and the assurance that what he intends to do will be correct. For him, it will be difficult to assume a task or commit to a decision without going through a reason-based research process. In contrast to Client 4, this person requires considerably more start-up time before he can articulate his opinions or engage in action.

The Knowing Process

In orienting himself through the thinking function, this client is guided in his decision and judgment-making process primarily by considerations of reason and logic. He knows things through research, discussion, debate, and analysis. This process is aided by sensing, a way of knowing that is also well developed in him. He relies upon sensing to help him in his process of data gathering, structuring, and organizing. Intuition, which in him is nearly as well-developed as sensing, helps him to see the possibilities inherent in a situation. This means that once he has constructed a well-reasoned, detailed, and structured analysis of his experience, he will also be prepared to consider the meaning and possibility contained in that situation, as well as modifications and changes to existing conditions. What is largely absent in this process is a conscious connection to feeling and emotion.

A profile that scores one of the ways of knowing substantially lower than the rest, alerts us to the possibility that the low-score function may be operating mostly outside the client's awareness. This does not mean that the client does not have access to this function. It does mean that the low-score function is one to which the client probably pays little attention in his process of knowing. In this case, feeling (15) ranks ten points lower than its closest neighbor (intuiting, 25), while the other functions have much more evenly distributed scores. What this indicates is that emotion, empathy, relational values, and subjective valuation based on personal values give way to other ways of judgment formation. The standards against which this client measures himself are largely abstract and external. He may have real difficulties with knowing his own feelings and articulating his emotions, or even considering them relevant. Tasks and objectives take precedence over relational and emotional concerns.

Differences in the Knowing Process

Clients 4 and 5 offer contrasting approaches to judgment formation. One begins with feeling and pays little attention to thinking; the other begins with thinking and pays little attention to feeling. As a result, their ethical stance, their morality, will be construed quite differently. Each offers us a different perspective as a basis for moral decision making. These two perspectives have been articulated in the work of Carol Gilligan and are summarized below.

Two Perspectives on Morality

One moral perspective is called a "morality of justice" and concerns itself with right action based in adherence to rules and principles. The other is a "morality of response and care" and concerns itself with right action based in an ability to respond in ways that care for and do not hurt others (Gilligan, 1982; Lyons, 1988).

Individuals grounded in a morality of justice judge themselves and others according to their ability to act fairly, without bias and in accordance with their principles. The underlying assumption is that the "good" is to be found in abstract ethical principles which transcend personal connections. Individuals grounded in a morality of response and care judge themselves and others in terms of their ability to care for others and maintain relationships. The underlying assumption is that the "good" is to be found in relatedness and is measured according to how successfully relatedness is maintained.

These two perspectives differ considerably in how they define the individual in relation to others, how they outline or "set up" moral problems, and how moral choices are considered and evaluated.

A morality of justice is premised on the belief that human beings are ultimately separate and autonomous in relation to each other and that relationships work best if they are reciprocal and if moral choices are mediated by rules that are fair — the same for all, and held in place by adherence to duties, obligations, and commitments outlined by the roles that we assume. From this perspective, moral problems arise out of competing rights or from the violation of rights, and are resolved by invoking impartial rules, principles, or standards, and by considering (1) one's role-related obligations, duties, or commitments, and (2) the accepted rules, standards, and principles for self, others, and society. The golden rule, "Do unto others as you would have them do unto you," serves to guide action. Moral decisions are evaluated by considering (1) how the decisions were considered and justified, i.e., how rational the decision was, and (2) how the invoked values, principles, or standards (especially those of reciprocity and fairness) were and are being maintained as a result of the decisions taken (Lyons, 1988, p. 35). Moral maturity is demonstrated by the ability to subordinate relationships to rules and rules to universal principles or human rights under the condition of blind impartiality (Gilligan, 1982).

A morality of response and care is premised on the belief that human beings are ultimately interdependent and connected to each other and that relationships work best if they are grounded in the act of caring for and about one another. Moral choices are mediated by understanding and the acceptance of one's responsibilities in a way that promotes the greatest good for all concerned. From this perspective, moral problems are construed as issues of relationship or response, and the concern is how to respond to others in their terms. The statement, "Do unto others as they would have you do unto them," guides action. When action is taken, the main consideration is the maintenance of the connections between the interdependent individuals involved, and the promotion of their welfare through preventing them from being harmed, or relieving them of their burdens, hurts, or suffering (Lyons, 1988, p. 35). The success or failure of one's intervention is evaluated by considering how things worked out, and whether relationships were maintained or restored and responsibilities acted upon. Moral maturity is demonstrated through the ability to maintain a complex network of human relationships, the acceptance of responsibility for others (including care of one's self), and that others are ultimately responsible for their own destiny (Gilligan, 1982).

These two perspectives offer very different ways of understanding "right action" and very different bases for deciding what is "good." It is important for the counsellor to understand and respect this difference and to take it into account when working with the feeling function. A client who premises his or her experience on thinking as a starting point, and who introduces feeling as an almost unconscious afterthought, will have a difficult time conceptualizing judgment formation as anything other than objective measurement against agreed-upon standards and rules. The idea that judgment formation may also be based on personal values could seem alien or "wrong" to a person strongly grounded in thinking as a way of knowing. For such a client, feeling is subordinated to reason, order, and "correctness," and thus a foray into the foreign territory of feeling may be threatening. The fear is that feeling will open the door to mere subjectivity and therefore relativistic chaos, in which there is no objective way to judge what is right. An entry into feeling is best negotiated carefully, with the counsellor paying deference to rationality, rationalization, and explanation until the client is convinced that feeling as a way of

knowing is useful, and is also persuaded that the subjective has value in relation to the objective.

Conversely, in working with someone who is strongly grounded in the feeling function, as is Client 4, the counsellor must recognize that feeling can overwhelm judgment at the expense of reflection. The client's investment in feeling can be so great that it can preclude the possibility of alternative ways of understanding experience. In either case, it is important for the counsellor to explore the underlying beliefs that structure and organize how the client situates himself in experience. Paying attention to ways of knowing can be immensely helpful in the work of deconstructing experience and understanding how to use emotional experience constructively.

How we communicate, both verbally and nonverbally (e.g., facial expression, body posture, gesture, presentation, context), offers useful clues to how we know ourselves and the world. The examples outlined in this chapter offer some insights into the integrative aspects of ways of knowing. The number of possible permutations that arise out of combining ways of knowing is limited only by the number of individuals who are willing to enter into constructing understandings in this way. The manner in which we have developed our ways of knowing has a major impact on how we understand our own emotional experience and that of others. In treating emotional experience as a resource rather than an outcome, we can begin by situating emotion in relation to ways of knowing. With this as our starting point, we can proceed in ways that respect each individual's unique relationship to emotional experience.

In Chapter 3, we will explore how the language of emotion signals the ways of knowing that an individual uses, as well as his or her evaluation of that experience.

Key Points

- The manner in which the counsellor has developed her own ways of knowing has a major impact on how she understands her own emotional experience and that of her clients.

- Before asking any client to engage in feeling work, the counsellor must first understand how that client relates to feeling.

- The client's "Ways of Knowing" Profile provides a useful map for entry into his or her world of experience.

- Successful feeling work depends on the counsellor's respect for the client's unique integration of ways of knowing. Premature demands for feeling can backfire.

The World in a Word

Underlying Premises

If we accept feeling as the way of knowing with which we discern and judge how and what we value, and we accept that the emotion-words with which we label or name our experiences inform us about our feeling judgments, then we can clarify our feeling judgments for ourselves and others through the words we use to describe our emotional experiences. Thus, each emotion can be viewed as a

> . . . characteristic set of our judgments and our desires, our intentions and our strategies. . . . In a sense, there are no individual emotions, but only a system of judgments from which we can abstract and simplify and identify certain

dominant patterns of judgment by using individual emotion names. (Solomon, 1983, p. 280)

Therefore, the vocabulary we use to describe what we feel is crucial to understanding our feelings. The words we choose are the windows to the worlds in which we live.

This notion — that there is a mutual dependency between the words we use and our experience of the world — is not new, but is nonetheless powerful. Wilhelm von Humboldt, a late-eighteenth and early-nineteenth century humanist and linguistic scholar, wrote that "because of the mutual dependency of thought and word, it is evident that languages [words] are not really means of representing the truth that has already been ascertained, but far more, means of discovering a truth not previously known" (cited in Edwards, 1967, p. 74).

Hans Georg Gadamer, a modern-day philosopher concerned with understanding how we form interpretations of experience, elaborated on von Humboldt's idea that our language view is our world view. He suggests that having words means having an orientation in the world. Our capacity for variety in orientations and understandings increases with an increased capacity for language (Gadamer, 1992, pp. 439-456). Therefore, the greater our ability to express ourselves in language, the greater is our capacity for freedom. Each new verbal understanding of a situation frees us from the oppression of being tied to one particular understanding of that situation. In coming to new terms with our experience (or even any terms at all), we rise above it to a certain extent and thereby come to understand it better. Mary Belenky (1986) and other feminist scholars have pointed out that the development of self and mind is closely linked to the development of voice, the ability to put into words what is being experienced.

Making Use of Words

In working with clients' emotional experience, we can orient ourselves to their world through an understanding of their (and our) ways of knowing as revealed by the "Ways of Knowing" Profile, and by carefully tuning in to their use of language. Preferences in ways of knowing reveal themselves in language.

Clients who prefer to start the ways of knowing process with *sensing* will communicate with directness, will tell us how things are, will command and instruct us, will state the facts. Their use of language will be literal. When talking about their experiences, they will describe, review, label, make observations, categorize, and report. They will sound authoritative, and on a bad day they can sound controlling and bossy.

Those who prefer to start with *thinking* will communicate more indirectly, with some hesitancy and with great attention to detail. They will not commit themselves to a particular version of their experience until they have worked through and verified all the possible angles. When talking about their experiences, they will offer carefully thought-through, reasoned analyses which they will support with well-formulated summaries of relevant examples. They will sound thoughtful and logical. On a bad day they can sound overly analytic, long-winded, and indecisive.

Clients who prefer to start with *feeling* will also communicate indirectly and with some hesitation, because they will be more involved with relating to the needs of others than with articulating their own needs. They will be able to say how they feel, but may hesitate to put their own feelings ahead of those of others. When talking, they will be concerned with sharing and relating, and will quite often discuss their experiences in terms of significant others in their lives. Their use of language will be metaphoric and descriptive. They will sound sensitive and caring. On a bad day they can sound like doormats for other people.

Those who prefer to start with *intuiting* will be lively and colorful in both their verbal use of language and in their nonverbal delivery. Sometimes words will not be enough, so they will rely on gesture and dramatization. As they speak, they are quite often brainstorming rather than expressing a well-formulated concept. They can easily change direction in midstream and make connections that appear self-evident to them, but wildly divergent to others. When talking about their experiences, they will tell vivid stories, not always strictly literal, because the effect rather than the facts is what is important. They have the ability to draw listeners in imaginatively and keep them enthralled. They will sound interesting. On a bad day they can come across as self-dramatizing attention seekers who like performing for an audience.

The action words or predicates that we use are useful indicators of our ways of knowing. The emotional adjectives we use, along with our action words, are helpful keys to entry into our personal lifeworlds. Attunement to the meanings embedded in a client's choice and use of language is invaluable in working with emotional experience. The counsellor can enter his client's lifeworld by listening so carefully that he can understand and speak her language well enough to reflect her way of knowing and her emotional experience back to her. Both counsellor and client can learn a great deal from this process about how the client actively organizes and constructs her experience.

This kind of understanding is key to self-conscious and self-directed participation in growth and change. Giving voice to one's self by finding the words that most accurately make one's world come to life is an empowering experience. As clients articulate their experiences, they externalize them for the listening counsellor and for their own listening self. With the counsellor as ally, they are heard and they become able to hear themselves. They are then no longer mutely and unconsciously captive in the undifferentiated flow of experience to which they are simply subject. They are now standing outside the articulated experience and listening in. This puts them in the position of being able to analyze their experience and reflect upon it, and therefore assess the experience and their own behavior in it.

From that vantage point, clients can become conscious of the kinds of choices they are making and of possible alternatives. Awareness of choice and alternatives is immensely helpful when it comes to taking charge of one's own behavior and one's own life. This is especially important when working with feeling as a way of knowing, because it is through feeling that we exercise the value judgments that motivate and guide our behavior.

It is entirely possible that we may be guided by values that we actually no longer wish to hold. We can recognize this only through becoming conscious of our values. Until then, we may

continue to fly under automatic pilot in a direction we may no longer wish to go, and fighting ourselves all the way. Careful listening to the language of feeling and emotion can help us bring our judgments and values to awareness, so that we can better understand them and more readily make choices about them.

Many of us possess an impoverished emotional vocabulary consisting of a few general terms that we use across many conditions. This limits our ability to use feeling as a way of knowing, and concurrently limits our own understanding of the ways in which we evaluate and judge our experience. In helping clients to name their emotional experience we help them to understand and communicate more aspects of their lifeworld. By offering them an expanded choice of words in this area, we offer them an expanded world. Two points are important in this process:

- Entry into the client's lifeworld is facilitated through paying respectful attention to his way of knowing. This makes it possible to work with feeling as a way of knowing in a way that makes sense to the client.

- Expansion of emotional experience is facilitated through expanding the emotional vocabulary. A client can be introduced to an expanded emotional vocabulary through the simple step of providing her with a vocabulary list like the one included here.

Using the Emotions Vocabulary List

The Emotions Vocabulary List that follows on pages 56-72 is organized into categories of words. The headings represent commonly used and well-known ways of describing particular experiences, while the words grouped together under these headings offer a variety of different and distinctive ways of specifying an emotion within that broad category. The underlying premise here is that the more specific we can be about our emotional experience, the better able we are to understand the meaning that experience has for us. As our emotional vocabulary expands, our use of feeling as a way of knowing becomes more practiced and more helpful and useful to us.

To introduce the Emotions Vocabulary List — and with it, the notion that emotions are an important resource in finding the meaning in our experience — the counsellor can ask the client to do the following simple exercise. This is an educative intervention that can be used one-to-one or with groups in workshops. Its primary purpose is to give clients the opportunity to (a) learn about their present emotions vocabulary, (b) expand upon that vocabulary, and (c) experiment with the effects of words on experience.

Step One in using feeling as a way of knowing is finding just the right emotion-word to describe the experience.

Emotions Vocabulary Exercise

The following directions are given to the client:

1. Read the list and check off each word that names an emotion that you have felt.

2. If you come across a word you do not know, look it up in a dictionary and decide whether it describes an experience that you have had but were not able to put into words before. What happens when you find ways to put your experience into words? Does anything change? Does anything make more sense?

3. Try describing an experience you have had — for which you already have emotion-words — with new emotion-words that are different from the ones you have habitually used. What, if anything, changes?

4. When you have completed this exercise, discuss with your counsellor anything you may have learned from it about emotion and about your own emotional experience.

Key Points

- The vocabulary we use to describe what we feel is crucial to understanding our feelings.

- In working with clients' emotional experience, we can orient ourselves to their world through understanding their (and our) ways of knowing by carefully tuning in to their (and our) use of language.

- Expansion of emotional experience is facilitated through expanding the emotional vocabulary.

- Step One in using feeling as a way of knowing is finding just the right emotion-word to describe the experience.

" I MUST BE GETTING OLD...
THIS MORNING I CAUGHT MYSELF
FEELING 'SPRIGHTLY'. "

Emotions Vocabulary List

SAD - DEPRESSED - DISCOURAGED

below par
bereaved
blue
broken-hearted
brooding
burned
cast down
cheerless
crestfallen
dejected
✓demolished
depressed
despondent
✓destroyed
disappointed
discouraged
downcast
downhearted
dreary

drooping
dull
forlorn
gloomy
glum
grief-stricken
grieved
✓heavy-hearted
hopeless
✓in the dumps
low
moody
✓moping
morose
mournful
oppressed
pained
pessimistic
sad

saddened
serious
solemn
somber
sorrowful
✓spiritless
tearful
troubled
unhappy
weary
woeful
✓wrecked

_____
_____
_____
_____
_____
_____

PLAYFUL - JOKING - WITTY

agreeable
amusing
approachable
✓breezy
brisk
chummy
clever
cosmopolitan
droll
easygoing
free and easy
✓frisky
frolicsome
fun-loving
funny
game
genial

good humored
✓half-serious
happy-go-lucky
hearty
hospitable
humorous
ingenious
✓jaunty
jesting
jocular
joking
jolly
jovial
✓lighthearted
lively
mirthful
mischievous

original
quick-witted
smart
sociable
sparkling
sportive
sprightly
spry
vivacious
_____
_____
_____
_____
_____
_____

57

MISERABLE - TROUBLED - HURT - FRUSTRATED

abused
aching
afflicted
aggrieved
awful
battered
bothered
burdened
clumsy
cramped
cut to the heart
desolate
despairing
destitute
disagreeable
displeased
disquieted
dissatisfied
distressed
disturbed
dreadful

harassed
hassled
hindered
horrible
hurt
imprisoned
loaded down
lost
lousy
miserable
mistreated
oppressed
pathetic
perturbed
piteous
poor
pressured
puzzled
racked
restless
ridiculous

suffering
swamped
throbbing
tormented
tortured
troubled
uneasy
unfortunate
ungainly
unhappy
unlucky
unsatisfied
unsure
upset
vexed
woeful
wounded
wretched
_____
_____
_____

foolish
fretful
frustrated
futile
gripped

rotten |
ruined |
sore |
stabbed |
strained |

INTERESTED - EXCITED

active
alert
aroused
attracted to
bustling
busy
delighted
demonstrative
eager
enlivened
enthusiastic
entranced

excited
expectant
fascinated
flustered
impatient
impressed with
incited to
interested in
involved
keyed up
quickened
spurred on

stimulated |
tantalized |
thrilled |
|
|
|
|
|
|

LONELY - FORGOTTEN - LEFT OUT

abandoned
alienated
alone
bereft
cast aside
deserted
discarded
disliked
disowned
estranged
excluded
forgotten
forsaken
friendless
hated
homeless

ignored
isolated
jilted
left out
loathed
lonely
lonesome
lost
neglected
ostracized
outcast
overlooked
rebuffed
rejected
scorned
secluded

separated
shunned
slighted
snubbed
stranded
uninvited
unwelcome
_____
_____
_____
_____
_____
_____
_____

ASHAMED - GUILTY - EMBARRASSED

abashed
accused
ashamed
awkward
blamed
branded
chagrined
cheapened
condemned
conscience-stricken

corrupt
debased
defiled
degraded
denounced
derided
disapproved of
disgraced
dishonored

disreputable
doomed
embarrassed
guilty
humbled
humiliated
in a bind
in a predicament
in trouble
judged
mortified
put down
rebuked
red-faced
regretful
remorseful
repentant
reprimanded
ridiculous

roasted
scandalized
sentenced
shamed
sheepish
silly
slammed
sorry
stigmatized
wrong

_____
_____
_____
_____
_____
_____
_____
_____

61

DISGUSTED - SUSPICIOUS

abhorrent
apathetic
arrogant
callous
cynical
derisive
despising
detesting
disgusted
displeased
distrustful
dogmatic
doubting
envious
grudging
hesitant

indifferent
jealous
loathing
mistrustful
nauseated
nonchalant
offended
pompous
presumptuous
queasy
repulsed
revolted
sickened
skeptical
sneering
suspicious

ANGRY - HOSTILE - ENRAGED - IRRITATED

aggravated
aggressive
agitated
angry
annoyed
aroused
belligerent
bitter
boiling
bristling
brutal
bullying
contrary
cool
cranky
critical
cross
cruel
disagreeable

displeased
enraged
exasperated
ferocious
fierce
fighting
fired up
frenzied
fretful
fuming
furious
harsh
hateful
heartless
hostile
incensed
indignant
inflamed
infuriated

irked
irritated
mad
mean
out of sorts
outraged
perturbed
provoked
pushy
quarrelling
raving
ready to explode
rebellious
resentful
revengeful
ruffled
spiteful
stern
stormy

ANGRY - HOSTILE - ENRAGED - IRRITATED (continued)

vehement
vindictive
violent
vicious

wrathful
_____
_____
_____

AFRAID - TENSE - WORRIED

afraid
agonized
alarmed
anxious
apprehensive
cautious
concerned
disturbed
dreading
fearful
fidgety
frightened
hesitant
ill at ease

in a cold sweat
jittery
jumpy
nervous
on edge
panicky
petrified
quaking
quivering
restless
scared
shaken
tense
terrified

trembling
troubled
uncomfortable
uneasy
wary
worried
_____
_____
_____
_____
_____
_____

HAPPY - ELATED - PEACEFUL - RELAXED

amused
at ease
blissful
bright
brilliant
buoyant
calm
carefree
charmed
cheerful
contented
delighted
ecstatic
elated
enchanted
enjoying
exalted

excellent
exhilarated
exulting
fantastic
fine
fit
flushed with success
full
glad
glorious
good
gratified
great
happy
in high spirits
inspired
joyous

jubilant
laughing
lighthearted
magnificent
majestic
marvellous
merry
optimistic
overjoyed
peaceful
pleasant
pleased
proud
rejoicing
relaxed
satiated
satisfied

HAPPY - ELATED - PEACEFUL - RELAXED (continued)

serene
smiling
splendid
sunny
superb
sweet

terrific
thrilled
tremendous
turned on
witty
wonderful

_____
_____
_____
_____
_____

CURIOUS - ABSORBED

absorbed
analytical
attentive
concentrating
considering
contemplative
curious
diligent
deliberating
engrossed

in a brown study
inquiring
inquisitive
investigating
occupied
pensive
pondering
preoccupied
questioning
reasoning

reflecting
searching
thoughtful
weighing

_____
_____
_____
_____

KIND - HELPFUL - LOVING - FRIENDLY - THANKFUL

admired
adorable
affectionate
agreeable
altruistic
amiable
amorous
appreciative
ardent
benevolent
big-hearted
brotherly
caring
charitable
cherished
Christian
comforting
compassionate
compatible

congenial
considerate
cooperative
cordial
dedicated
devoted
diligent
doting
earnest
empathic
fair
faithful
fond
forgiving
friendly
gallant
generous
gentle
genuine

giving
good
gracious
grateful
helpful
honest
honorable
humane
idolizing
indebted to
involved
just
kind
longing for
long-suffering
loving
mellow
merciful
mindful

KIND - HELPFUL - LOVING - FRIENDLY - THANKFUL (continued)

neighborly	sensitive	trustful
nice	sharing	understanding
obliging	soft-hearted	unselfish
open	straightforward	warm-hearted
optimistic	sympathetic	————
passionate	tender	————
patient	thankful	————
praiseful	thoughtful	————
respectful	tolerant	————
rewarded	treasured	

VIGOROUS - STRONG - CONFIDENT

able-bodied	firm	sharp
accomplished	fit	skillful
adequate	forceful	smart
adventurous	fortunate	spirited
assured	gifted	stable
blessed	hardy	strong
bold	healthy	sturdy

brave
brawny
capable
clever
competent
confident
courageous
daring
deft
determined
durable
dynamic
effective
efficient
encouraged
energetic
equal to the task
favored
fearless

important
in control
intelligent
keen
lion-hearted
lucky
manly
mighty
nervy
peppy
potent
powerful
promising
prosperous
qualified
robust
secure
self-confident
self-reliant

suited
successful
sure
together
tough
triumphant
victorious
vigorous
virile
well-off
well-suited
wise
_____
_____
_____
_____
_____
_____
_____

CONFUSED - SURPRISED - ASTONISHED

aghast
amazed
appalled
astonished
astounded
awed
awestruck
baffled
bewildered
bowled over
breathless
confounded
confused
dazed
dazzled
disconcerted
dismayed
disrupted

disturbed
dumbfounded
electrified
flabbergasted
gripped
horrified
impressed
in doubt
jarred
jolted
muddled
nonplussed
overpowered
overwhelmed
perplexed
puzzled
ruffled
shocked

speechless
staggered
startled
struck
stunned
stupefied
surprised
taken aback
uncertain
_____
_____
_____
_____
_____

WEAK - DEFEATED - SHY - BELITTLED

all in
at the mercy of
bashful
belittled
bent
broken down
chickenhearted
cowardly
crippled
crushed
decrepit
defeated
defective
deflated
demoralized
disabled
done for
drowsy
dwarfed
exhausted

failing
fatigued
feeble
fragile
frail
haggard
harassed
helpless
hungry
imperfect
impotent
inadequate
incapable
incapacitated
incompetent
ineffective
inefficient
inept
inferior
infirm

insecure
insulted
jeered at
laughed at
made small
maimed
meek
mocked
nagged
needy
neglected
nerveless
no good
obsolete
open to attack
paralyzed
powerless
puny
put down
run down

71

WEAK - DEFEATED - SHY - BELITTLED (continued)

scoffed at
scorned
shaky
shattered
shy
small
sneered at
spent
strained
strengthless
tearful
timid
tired
troubled

unable
underestimated
underrated
unfit
unqualified
unsure of oneself
unworthy
useless
valueless
vulnerable
walked on
washed up
weak
whipped

worn out
worthless
_____
_____
_____
_____
_____

— Reproduced, with permission, from R. Vance Peavy (1977), *Empathic Listening Workbook*. Victoria, B.C.: Adult Counselling Project, University of Victoria.

Unpacking the Meanings in Emotional Experience: A Six-Step Strategy

Step One: Naming the Experience

Once we have chosen the word that most accurately describes our emotional experience, we are ready to unpack the meanings embedded in that word. Choosing the word is the first step. That gives the emotional experience a name and thereby frames it.

Language has the quality of delimiting experience because it fixes an experience as "this" and not some other thing. When I call something by this name and not some other, I have placed a strategic limitation upon it in terms of what it means to me. Naming is powerful. Donald Schon (1987), an educator interested in how practitioners make sense of their experience, suggests: "Through the complementary acts of naming and framing, [we] select things for attention and organize them, guided by an apperception (an understanding of something new in terms of previous experience) that gives coherence and sets a direction for action" (p. 4). Through naming we convey identity, we appropriate, we make real, and we validate. With regard to emotional experience, naming is important because, as well as permitting entry into our individual worlds of experience, it is the first step toward personal meaning making in understanding one's experience.

Step Two: Physically Locating the Experience

Relevant also to the appropriation and ownership of our emotional experience is locating it in our bodies. As we learned in Chapter 1, neurological and physiological arousal are definitely part of emotional experience. Our bodies provide us with rich and detailed information about our emotions, and while emotion can neither be reduced to nor explained in terms of our neurological and physiological arousal, that arousal serves us well by alerting us to the fact that we are in the midst of an emotional process.

In engaging with our emotional experience and unpacking its meanings, it is therefore helpful to work with our bodies. If we are able to pinpoint the bodily locus of our emotions we can use that information to refine further our understanding of our emotional experience. For example, if I allow that I use feeling as the way of knowing that orients me in my experience (for or against, positive or negative, yes or no), and I elaborate this valuation by naming it with emotion-words like "anxious" or "excited," "irritated" or "amused," and then I locate my experience in my body as anxious in the pit of my stomach, excited higher up in the chest around my heart, irritated in my shortness of breath and my flushed face, amused in the corners of my mouth and so on, I begin to develop a map of my emotions that can help me in two ways: (1) I can distinguish one emotion from another and therefore differentiate my experience; and (2) I can work positively with my body should I wish to change my emotional experience.

Let us recall Paul Ekman, the psychologist discussed in Chapter 1. He was able to initiate feeling by choice and affect emotion with conscious manipulation of facial expression, gesture, and posture. In so doing, he demonstrated to us that we can use feeling with intention and call up emotion at will. He used his body to help both with understanding emotion and with choosing emotion. We can do the same. Through knowing our bodies and working with our neurological and physiological systems we can, of our own accord, bring feeling as way of knowing to bear on our experience. But to do this with precision, we must make another distinction: we must differentiate between sensation and feeling.

AS HE REACHED FOR THE DOOR-KNOB, RON NOTICED THAT THE OPPRESSIVE SENSE OF DOOM AND FOREBODING HAD LEFT THE PIT OF HIS STOMACH AND WAS NOW LOCATED SQUARELY AT HEAD-LEVEL.

Feeling and Sensing Distinguished

In Chapter 3, we learned to distinguish between feeling and emotion, and found that feeling is the active process of making value judgments in the midst of experience while emotion is the summing up of those judgments. Now we will add a further dimension to this process, that of differentiating between feeling and sensation. It is common to refer to feeling and sensing as if they were very much the same processes. However, we have already seen (pp. 18-20) that as ways of knowing, feeling and sensing are quite different. While feeling organizes and judges according to personal values, sensing is the immediate recording of sights, sounds, smells, tastes, and touch impressions. Through sensing, we record the physiological actualities of experience. But because feeling and emotion are so interwoven with physiological and neurological information and response, we tend to experience our sensing as if it were part and parcel of feeling and emotion, and therefore find ourselves equating feeling with sensation.

This is reflected in our use of language. Without wondering about what we actually mean, we say things like: "I feel cold, I feel hungry, I feel tired," thereby suggesting that we have made a value judgment about the conditions we find ourselves in. In fact, we are describing sensations we are experiencing. Sensing is factual; feeling is evaluative. If we confuse the two, we could mistakenly confuse a fact with an evaluation, and find ourselves believing that we are dealing with facts when we are actually dealing with judgments. An individual I worked with provided me with a very graphic and very useful illustration of this point.

Case Study

Sharon was a client in a special program for abuse survivors where I taught communication and life skills and monitored clients' progress through individual counselling sessions. As I worked with her, I used both the "Ways of Knowing" Profile and the Six-Step Strategy for unpacking meaning in emotional experience. As mentioned previously, understanding individual preferences and priorities in ways of knowing, and being aware where feeling falls in the sense-making process, are extremely useful — especially when dealing with a client's emotional experience.

Sharon's "Ways of Knowing" Profile scored as follows: sensing, 19; thinking, 24; feeling, 32; intuiting, 25. This score suggests that her starting point with any experience would be to judge it according to her personal values. It also suggests that she relies more heavily on feeling as a way of knowing than on the other three functions, and further that she relies least on sensing as a way of knowing. Indeed, she may not be particularly aware of sensory information as separate from feeling judgments.

Given that Sharon begins her process with feeling, she will know almost instantly whether she accepts or rejects the conditions she finds herself in. Her likes and dislikes will be apparent to her immediately, as will either her willingness or her unwillingness to proceed. Her intuitive function (the capacity to discover the meanings and possibilities inherent in a given situation) and her thinking function (the capacity for reaching decisions through logical, step-by-step deliberations) work closely together, but are likely to be influenced strongly, and perhaps even overruled, by her feeling evaluations. Her sensing function (the capacity to notice sensory details and to create order through attention to particulars) is not one Sharon is likely to make use of without encouragement.

Sharon's inclination was to make no distinction between feeling and sensing, and to treat sense information as if it were synonymous with feeling. This meant she dealt with her feeling evaluations as facts rather than judgments.

In working with Sharon, it was important to (a) acknowledge and explore carefully the full meaning of her emotions, and (b) help her to separate evaluation (feeling) from fact (sensing).

Before Sharon used the approach of naming and locating her emotional experience and before she was able to distinguish between feeling (the making of evaluative judgments) and sensing (the immediate recording of sensory information), she used to have difficulty with weight gain. In order to help her make sense out of her experience, I asked her about her eating patterns. She reported that she ate whenever she was hungry, and that at certain times she felt much more hungry than others. I asked her what her signals for eating were. She replied that she hadn't really thought about it, but that it had to do with feeling hungry. I asked her to describe to me in a more detailed way what she was calling "hungry". Upon reflection, she thought that whenever she experienced sensations in the center of her body around the area of her stomach, she was calling that "hunger" and was eating as a consequence. In other words, she was naming the sensations that she had "hunger" and acting upon the naming. I asked her if these sensations could possibly be called anything else. When she paid more attention to how she was naming her experience, she began to notice that two events were occurring, not just one.

One event involved the tightening of her muscles and an empty feeling located just to the left of center in the upper middle of her belly. This she named hunger. Hunger is a sensation involving the complex interaction of a number of physiological signals. It is a concrete, fact-based experience. The other event involved a kind of pulling in of her stomach muscles and the sensation of knotting more in the center of her belly. This she named anxiety.

When we are anxious, we have made a decision that the thing we are facing holds some kind of threat for us. Our central nervous system may be involved in our decision process, but it is really our feeling evaluation of the conditions we find ourselves in that helps us to name our experience as anxiety. When Sharon found that she was able to distinguish between sensation on the one hand and the feeling-emotion decision process on the other, she was able to feed herself when she was hungry, and go further into her evaluative process of the conditions under which she experienced anxiety when these occurred. From then on, she ate when she was actually hungry and investigated her evaluative process when she was anxious. As a consequence of eating only when she was truly hungry, she was able to maintain a weight that was acceptable to her.

Until she distinguished between the feeling-emotion process and sensing, Sharon was confusing the taking in of sense information with the making of evaluative judgments. As a consequence, she was treating her evaluative judgments as sensory facts and eating when she was both anxious and hungry. She did this largely because, generally speaking, her physiological signals were similar under both conditions, and she had not as yet learned to differentiate her sense experience from her evaluative experience through the process of attending to it, naming and locating it

When she did do this, she very quickly noticed what the differences were and found this knowledge helpful. She could now distinguish sensation (hunger) from emotion (anxiety). She could map anxiety as a cluster of sensations located in the center of her belly. Finally, she could work positively with her bodily feedback, meaning that she could: (a) feed herself when hungry, and (b) further evaluate conditions when anxious.

To help her with learning more about her anxiety, we went on with our process of unpacking the meanings in emotional experience. I asked Sharon to describe a time when she felt anxious. Sharon told me that she often felt anxious on Sunday evenings when she was preparing for her week at school and work. She had recently decided to upgrade her training so that she could return to work, and was attending a retraining program that involved attending classes two days per week and going to a work experience placement three days per week. One weekly program requirement was to plan her week in advance with the help of a day book. On Sunday evenings she became anxious as she tried to plan the week ahead, and often felt overwhelmed as she sat with her day book and made out her schedule.

We knew from our earlier discussion that Sharon was able to label her emotion as anxiety and was able to locate her anxiety in the center of her belly. Having followed the first and second step of the strategy for unpacking the meaning of emotional experience, we were ready to go on. To learn about the next four steps, let us follow Sharon as she continues to unpack the meanings in her emotional experience.

Step Three: Hearing Our Self-Talk

When we are in the midst of emotional experience (or indeed at any time), it is not uncommon to engage in self-talk. Self-talk is the expression of the thoughts we have about our experiences in the form of words, phrases, and sentences that we repeat to ourselves. Sometimes it takes the form of internal dialogues that we conduct with ourselves or with others in our minds. In any case, self-talk often accompanies our experience. In some ways self-talk is "mental muzak" — our personally generated background noise. It is so much a part of our habitual way of dealing with experience, especially emotional experience, that we may not even be aware of the kinds of things we tell ourselves. Over time, most of us become so used to our own continuous self-talk that we are no longer even conscious of the messages we give ourselves. However, the effect of self-talk can be quite dramatic.

Cognitively based therapists (Beck,1967; Ellis, 1988; de Sousa, 1990; Mahoney, 1991) have demonstrated that there is a clear connection between the kinds of things we tell ourselves and the feeling evaluations we make. Research with clients who suffer from depression, even physiologically based depression, has shown that recovery depends upon the client's ability to utter positive self-talk (Rush, 1977, cited in Davison & Neale, 1982, pp. 256-257). Negative self-talk blocks recovery. The effects of positive and negative internal monologues are currently being studied in the field of healing and health. Findings published to date (Schmale & Iker, 1971; Seligman, 1975; Pelletier, 1977; Rossi, 1986) show that there is a notable connection between the ability to construct positive internal monologues and healing. Given the large body of research that supports the importance of self-talk, we can safely assume that what we say to ourselves matters.

I asked Sharon to tune in to the kinds of things she was saying to herself as she went about the business of planning her weekly schedule on Sunday evenings. Here is what she heard herself say:

"Oh god, how I hate sitting here planning the week; there's never enough time for the things I have to do anyway. Planning is a waste of time; something unexpected always comes up, so why

SOMEWHERE, DEEP DOWN, A PART OF SPEEDY STILL COULD NOT BELIEVE HE WAS REALLY MAN'S BEST FRIEND.

do I bother? I can't do this; there are too many things I can't control going on. Look at all the things they expect us to do; it's too much! I hate schedules. People should be free. Why do we have to come in with our week planned? They don't know what it's like to juggle school and work and caring for a small child. I don't know if I can do this."

Her self-talk articulated her assessment that advance planning of her weekly activities is a negative experience. Her internal monologue raises two issues. The first is that of her dislike for the whole notion of advance planning. The second, which may be more deeply seated than the first, is her conviction that she is unable to do the task. Knowing this is instructive for both client and counsellor. Internal issues underlying behavior can now be addressed. In order to further our understanding of Sharon's process, we moved to the next step in the enterprise of unpacking the meanings of her emotional experience — that of seeing the images she was projecting onto it.

Step Four: Seeing the Internal Images We Project upon Experience

We not only engage in self-talk on a continuous basis, we also continuously engage in the making of internal pictures. Along with our "mental muzak," we are constantly producing images or "home movies" of past experience and future expectation which we project upon the present.

Philosophers and psychologists have long been concerned with the connection between mental imagery and cognitive processes. The notion that cognition has sensory content and that it may be impossible to engage in cognitive activity without creating imagery was raised many years ago by both John Locke (1690) and George Berkeley (1710). The accuracy of the claim that visualization is always a part of cognition has been debated and discussed through the centuries, and no ultimate conclusion has been reached. However, there is agreement that, while it may be possible on some level to have cognition without immediately discernible visual content, no cognition takes place without the physiological, and therefore sensory, engagement of the person involved (Heidbreder, 1961). Cognition is not passive, but active. What we do when we engage in cognitive processes has a bearing on our experience. The images we make are part of our active engagement in cognition. These images can be treated as useful resources that we can study in our quest for insight into the ways in which we structure and organize our experience.

This knowledge has been used effectively by many writers and trainers in the fields of self-help, personal growth, and healing, where books on visualization abound (Simonton & Simonton, 1978; Peale, 1982; Odle, 1990). The thesis is that the visual contents of experience, like the auditory and the physiological contents, give shape and structure to our lives. Thus, it follows that the more actively we can become aware of both the images we project and the impact of these images upon our experience and our actions, the more able we are to:

1. Realize that what we superimpose or project upon experience dramatically influences that experience;

2. Understand that our projections are actually resources that give us insight into past experience and future expectations, and show us on what we are basing the structure and organization of our experience;

3. Consciously choose how to influence and shape our experience by projecting more positively.

With this knowledge in mind, let us return to Sharon. After asking Sharon to tune in to her self-talk, I asked her to look at the images she was projecting with regard to planning her weekly schedule on Sunday evenings. Here is what she saw:

- Sharon trying to get herself and her three-year-old daughter out of the house in time to catch the bus, while the child plays with her toys and refuses to cooperate with getting dressed.

- Sharon sitting down at her kitchen table to work, and staring off into the distance because she is so tired that she just can't concentrate.

- Sharon facing her teacher with her homework not done, and not wanting to look at her teacher's face.

- Sharon during the time before she attended the retraining program, sitting quietly on a Sunday evening watching television while her child sleeps.

Her images sketched out both past experience and future expectation. Based on what had gone before, she now expected that she would be prevented from keeping to a schedule by the demands of parenting and her own fatigue. She also expected to have difficulty facing her teacher with her homework not done and saw herself at a time when she was able to relax because there were no Sunday night scheduling demands in her life. Taken together, Sharon's "home movie" projected the anticipation that she would neither adequately make nor keep her schedule and that things were more relaxing when this was not a task she had to face.

We now had even more raw material to round out the work of unpacking the meaning of her experience with planning a schedule. With self-talk and projections in hand, we proceeded to Step Five.

Step Five: Making Interpretations

As human beings, we are constantly in the business of making interpretations of our experience. The word interpret means "to explain or tell the meaning of, to present in understandable terms, to conceive in the light of individual belief, judgment, or circumstance, to construe, to represent, . . . to bring to realization by means of performance" (Webster, 1975). Feeling and emotion are central to this interpretive process. (Recall the discussion in Chapter 1, pp. 10-16, where the point was made that feeling is constitutive of experience, the source of meaning and value, and the prime mover in the interaction of thought and feeling.) Ultimately, feeling is a meaning-making process which, although it happens almost instantaneously, is exquisitely complex and subtle and involves the total engagement of the feeling person — the author of the feeling experience. In unpacking the embedded meanings in feeling and emotion we must ask ourselves, "How am I interpreting this experience? What do I think this means?"

Naming and locating our experience, tuning in to our self-talk, and looking closely at our projections are the first four steps that help us to answer the above questions. Here the fifth and summative step begins to take shape, and an overall conceptualization emerges.

What emerged for Sharon was an overwhelming sense of inadequacy and anger out of which she was constructing herself as helpless in the face of forces she considered more powerful than herself: teachers, the demands of working life, and her child, all of which appeared to her to be factors out of her control. When she answered the question, "How am I interpreting this experience?" she responded: "Making schedules puts me in touch with how out of control I feel and how I hate any controls that I see as imposed upon me by others. This puts me in touch with my inability to make my life into something that I want it to be."

When she answered the question, "What do I think this means?" she responded: "I think that having to make and keep a schedule, especially one that I have to show an authority figure like a teacher, is going to show people how 'untogether' my life really is, and that makes me feel helpless and angry at the same time."

Her anxiety — an emotion described in Webster (1975) as "painful or apprehensive uneasiness of mind, usually over an impending or anticipated ill" — began to make a great deal of sense, given her interpretation of the meaning of schedule making. Having used feeling as the way of knowing used to discern and judge, Sharon had judged herself as inadequate and her situation as threatening because it was certain to expose her as incapable of taking control.

That summation left us with one final step to take in the process of using emotional experience constructively: that of questioning our interpretations and creating alternatives.

Step Six: Questioning and Reframing Our Interpretations

Once we have unpacked the meanings embedded in emotional experience, we find ourselves in a good position to ask some questions about how we have constructed and organized our experience. With these six steps comes the discovery that we ourselves have made or created meaning. Meaning does not reside outside ourselves in the conditions of our lives, as we so often believe; rather, it resides in our unique and subjective evaluations. Furthermore, as we engage in the making of meaning, we also engage in anticipating or predicting outcomes with regard to the conditions in which we find ourselves. For example, Sharon anticipated that she would be unmasked as inadequate and out of control as a result of not making and keeping a schedule. Instead, she discovered that her interpretations and the predictions she was making as a result of them were her own unique and personal assessments, not absolute facts. In learning this she also learned that she could reframe what she herself had framed in the first place.

As we undertake the process of questioning and reframing our assessments, we are in fact enlarging our feeling experience by introducing two more ways of knowing into the process: intuiting (the capacity to rework existing conditions and find potential and possibility) and thinking (the problem-solving function that analyzes and deliberates). By asking ourselves: "Is the interpretation I have formed the only one possible under the circumstances? Are there other ways in which I might interpret this experience?" and "How many different interpretations can I come up with?", we enlist our intuition in a search for new possibilities.

Having created alternative interpretations, we may then enlist our thinking function to help us with a systematic analysis of them by asking ourselves, "Do any of these make logical sense to me? Do I judge any of them as valid, and if so, why?" As we enter into the questioning process, we also enter into a new and expanded creative process. We begin experimenting with sense making in a way that allows us to take charge of the process consciously and purposefully. When Sharon asked herself "Is the interpretation I've formed the only one possible under the circumstances?", she started to nod and say, "Yes, of course; I really can't make scheduling work." Given that her first inclination is to make strong feeling judgments and hold these with conviction, this response was not surprising. But then she paused and began to wonder about the way in which she was evaluating both herself and her circumstances. She moved to the next two questions: "Are there any other ways in which I might interpret this experience? How many different interpretations can I come up with?"

At first she had some difficulty with the notion that she might judge the situation differently, because she had built up such a strong antipathy to the task of scheduling. Remembering that a morality of care and response (pp. 42-46), which concerns itself with understanding and relating compassionately to others, often accompanies feeling as a way of knowing, I asked, "If your best friend had trouble with scheduling, would your only possible interpretation be that she is inadequate and 'untogether'?" This question gave Sharon pause. She immediately saw that she would neither judge nor limit her friend in the way she had judged and limited herself. She then allowed herself to experiment with alternative interpretations by pretending that her best friend felt the same way about schedules, and that she was brainstorming other possibilities with her friend. This allowed the following process to take place:

The first interpretation she questioned was the notion that not keeping a schedule meant she was incapable of being in control of her life. She decided that at worst, not making and keeping a schedule meant that under present circumstances, scheduling didn't work all that well for her. This decision released her from the notion that scheduling was a measure of her own (and perhaps others') capacity for self-determination, which is how she had been construing scheduling thus far.

She then questioned the notion that she was helpless and inadequate, both when it came to scheduling and to facing the teacher whose disapproval she anticipated. First, she re-evaluated her teacher's possible reactions. Based on previous experiences with this teacher, she decided that it was highly unlikely her teacher would communicate disapproval with regard to an incomplete schedule. It appeared to her that her teacher might express concern, and that she might ask Sharon some questions about what was making scheduling difficult, but that this would not be done in a disapproving way. She then speculated that if her teacher were to treat her with concern rather than disapproval, this would mean that she had nothing to fear from her teacher.

Next, she re-evaluated the direct connection she had drawn between inadequacy and helplessness and making and keeping a schedule. She spent some time wondering where the idea had come from that scheduling somehow reflected self-control and personal adequacy. Nothing immediately leapt to mind, but eventually she decided that so much of everyday life is governed by timetables and schedules that she had come to believe that there was some deeper value attached to staying within the frameworks we construct for ourselves. She compared this to staying inside the lines when coloring. Although she herself didn't attach all that much value to staying inside the lines when coloring or even to coloring (she preferred using color expressively and having a free hand when drawing), she had learned very soon in her primary school life that staying inside the lines was approved of, as was being on time and getting things done according to the clock. Her discomfort with this way of thinking, her dislike for it and her expectation of disapproval should she not meet accepted standards, dated back to early school life.

When Sharon realized that much of what she was experiencing was a frustrating carry-over from childhood, a time when she had little control and needed the support and approval of powerful adults, she decided to bring her expectations of self and others up to date. She decided that under present conditions she had much more power than she had given herself credit for.

First of all, she was now an adult. She had chosen both motherhood and her retraining program. She wanted to parent her child and she wanted to learn the skills she needed to get the kind of job that would pay her well enough to look after herself and her child independently. Rather than seeing herself as out of control, she saw herself as choosing to do challenging things that were sometimes hard to accomplish.

As a consequence of exploring her construal of herself, she shifted from framing herself as helpless and inadequate in relation to the demands of powerful others to formulating herself as an individual who sometimes found it difficult to meet all aspects of the challenges she had chosen for herself. This change in orientation to self led to a change in how she positioned herself with regard to those tasks and encounters of daily life that she found anxiety provoking.

Anxiety became a signal for her to wonder about how she was structuring her experience and to examine the conditions in which she found herself in order to uncover the underlying meanings embedded in the situation. Eventually, she noticed that for her, there was often a connection between anxiety and momentary forgetfulness of her own ability to notice alternatives, solve problems, and make decisions in her own best interest. This in turn was tied to her preference for feeling as a way of knowing, which sometimes prompted her to forget possibility and analysis and omit sense-based facts. Remembering her own power in the face of frustration, anger and threat became Sharon's new challenge. Making and keeping schedules became a question of choices and priorities rather than a battle with authority figures and clocks.

This process of unpacking the meanings that we deposit in experience can lead to an insightful and useful reorganization of the ways in which we know ourselves, others, and the conditions of our lives. If we treat feeling and emotion as helpful and informative sources of knowledge and understanding that are an integral and active part of our sense-making process rather than mere reactive phenomena, we enter into experience as active participants, not passive recipients. For Sharon, this recognition facilitated an empowering change: first it helped her to maintain an acceptable weight, and gradually to construct herself as a capable adult.

Key Points

- Feeling is an orienting function that we use to situate ourselves in experience relative to our values.

- Feeling guides us in the formation of judgments.

- The emotions that we recognize, name, and apply to our experience as a result of how we have valued it through feeling, inform us about the feeling judgments we have made.

- Feeling is a way of knowing that works in concert with the three other ways of knowing: sensing, thinking, and intuiting. Each performs a different function in creating understanding and making sense out of human experience.

- In order to work effectively with feeling as a way of knowing, the counsellor must take the time to understand how a client uses feeling in relation to the other ways of knowing. Success depends upon both the counsellor's and the client's understanding of how the client relates to feeling, before embarking on any feeling work.

Once the above points are understood, counsellor and client can begin working constructively with emotional experience by using the Six -Step Strategy for unpacking the meanings in emotional experience.

Appendix A: Warm-up Exercise

The objective of the following exercise, which was developed by Sheila Moult (1989), is to help the client recognize that he is an active agent in his emotional experience, and thereby help him to acknowledge his own power and capability.

The exercise can be done with clients individually or in a group as a warm-up prior to introducing the Six-Step Strategy for working with emotional experience.

Introduction

The Six-Step Strategy that we will use for unpacking the meanings in our emotional experience consists of the following steps:

1. Name the experience
2. Physically locate the experience
3. Hear our self-talk
4. See the internal images we project upon experience
5. Make interpretations
6. Question and reframe our interpretations

In order to get some feeling for this strategy, please complete the following sentences. Then "unpack" the meaning of your experience by exploring each of your answers in relation to the above six steps. This means that in each case you name the emotion, locate this emotion in your body, hear what you are telling yourself about this experience, see the images you are projecting onto this experience, note how you are interpreting the experience (i.e., what does it all mean), then question and reframe your interpretation in order to explore other possibilities.

Practice Scenarios

1. When I spill my coffee, I feel...
2. When I get a parking ticket, I feel...
3. When someone gives me a flower, I feel...

4. When I miss a bus, I feel...
5. When I crack a joke and people laugh, I feel...
6. When I hear the phone ring, I feel...
7. When I make myself a good dinner, I feel...
8. When I see the crocuses opening, I feel...
9. When the teacher corrects me, I feel...
10. When I do someone a favor, I feel...
11. When the boss wants to see me, I feel...
12. When the phone stops ringing before I get it, I feel...

These twelve scenarios represent common, everyday occurrences during which we often simply take our emotions for granted. They are used here as a starting point for practicing the Six-Step Strategy for unpacking meaning in emotional experience. Through them we can learn more about how meanings and values are embedded in even the most ordinary experiences.

Appendix B: Summary of the Six-Step Strategy

Step One: Naming the Experience

The words we choose to describe our experiences help us to organize and structure that experience and put us in touch with the evaluations and judgments we have made. These words provide the openings or entry points to the meanings we have deposited in experience. It is important, therefore, to find the best emotional label to name and summarize our emotional experience accurately.

Key Questions:

- Can you describe what you are feeling? What is it like? What would you like to do?

- Can you name the emotion that best describes your experience?

- Are there other names that also apply?

Step Two: Physically Locating the Experience

Because neurological and physiological arousal are definitely part of emotional experience, our bodies provide us with rich and detailed information about the state of that arousal. The more familiar we become with the meanings we attach to particular physiological signals, the better we are at understanding and working with our emotional experiences.

Key Questions:

- Where in your body is this emotional experience located?

- What physical signals are you receiving while you are having this emotional experience?

Step Three: Hearing Our Self-Talk

There is a clear connection between the things we tell ourselves and our feeling evaluations. Our self-talk further articulates and expands upon the feeling judgments we make. Hearing what we are telling ourselves helps us to learn more about how we are structuring our experience.

Key Questions:

- What are you telling yourself as you engage in this emotional experience?

- Are there any words or phrases that you hear yourself repeating in the midst of this experience?

- Is what you are hearing spoken by your own voice, or someone else's? (Self-talk formulated as "I" statements usually indicates the speaker's own voice. "You"-statement self-talk may indicate internalized comments originally imposed on the speaker by others. It can be fruitful to explore the source of "you" statements.)

Step Four: Seeing the Internal Images We Project upon Experience

The visual images we project or superimpose upon experience show us how we shape present experience with imagery that we carry with us from the past and carry over into future expectation. Becoming aware of these projections helps us gain insight into how we shape and influence experience through projection.

Key Questions:

- What do you see in front of you as you are in the midst of this experience? (Are you visualizing yourself in any way — in the past, in the future?)

- What do you imagine will happen?

- How do things look to you? (Describe visually.)

Step Five: Making Interpretations

Ultimately, feeling is an interpretive process. It is a process of evaluation, often experienced as instantaneous and spontaneous, that involves the total engagement of the person. Knowing and understanding our interpretations puts us in a position to work with this process consciously.

Key Questions:

- How are you interpreting this experience?

- What do you think this experience means (about yourself, about the others involved, about what will happen)?

- How are you assessing this experience (situation)?

- Overall, what judgments (evaluations) have you made (about yourself, others, the situation)?

Step Six: Questioning and Reframing Our Interpretations

Once we have unpacked the meanings we have deposited in our experiences, we find ourselves in a good position to ask ourselves some questions about how we have structured and organized that experience. This questioning of our interpretation allows us to enter into the process of analyzing and reframing.

Key Questions:

- Is the interpretation you have made the only one possible under the circumstances?

- Are there any other ways in which you might interpret this experience?

- How many different interpretations can you come up with? Do any of your new interpretations seem logically possible? Do they appear to be valid?

- What other alternatives and possibilities exist here?

Conclusion

As a counsellor and teacher, I have worked with feeling as a way of knowing and the Six-Step Strategy in a variety of settings. I have been able to use the strategy effectively with clients in individual counselling sessions, with recovery groups in communications and life skills training programs, with professionals in career retraining and professional development seminars, and with university students learning to counsel others. In each situation I have found it useful to keep the following points in mind.

Creating a Shared Understanding of Feeling and Emotion

At the outset, it is important to come to an understanding of how those I am working with regard feeling and emotion. As discussed in Chapter 1, over time, feeling and emotion have been variously regarded as involuntary neurophysiological responses, as instincts and psychic energy, as expressions caused by antecedent events, and as perceptions that organize activity. We all have theories, ideas, and assumptions about feeling and emotion that affect how we deal with emotional experience. It is helpful to articulate and explore these notions with clients and students before introducing feeling as a way of knowing and the Six-Step Strategy. The ways in which we understand feeling and emotion, both personally and socioculturally, guide our responses, expectations, and actions in this realm. We are best able to incorporate new and different ways of understanding these experiences into our response repertoire if our familiar responses are articulated, acknowledged, appreciated, and connected to these new and as yet unfamiliar approaches.

With Groups or Classes

When I am working with a group or a class to create a shared understanding of feeling and emotion, we engage in brainstorming: i.e., we ask the question, "What is emotion?" and create a comprehensive list of everyone's theories and beliefs with regard to this topic. Invariably the above-mentioned construals of emotion come up, and invariably, emotion and feeling are seen as synonymous. Because this is a brainstorming session (which means that all ideas are recorded and no idea is rejected until all possibilities have been exhausted), everyone's ideas are noted, and each is discussed and explored in turn. During the discussion, the counsellor (or teacher, or facilitator) also introduces her or his own concepts into the discussion and makes connections between the ideas presented by students or group members and the counsellor's own. This allows for the articulation of a comprehensive and, for most people, much expanded understanding of emotion. It also creates an opening for the introduction of two new ideas: (1) that feeling can be understood as a way of knowing and (2) that a distinction can be made between feeling and emotion.

At this point, the material presented in Chapters 1 and 2 of this guidebook can be integrated into the group discussion. Clients and students can be invited to explore their ways of knowing preferences and can be introduced to the distinction between feeling and emotion. That discussion leads to the next point, that of the impact of language on our emotional life. This brings in the material discussed in Chapter 3 and sets the stage for working with the Six-Step Strategy as described in Chapter 4.

The timing of the above discussion in groups and classes depends upon choices made by the instructor/facilitator, or in some cases the mutual agreement reached by group and facilitator, with regard to when this topic best fits into the course or the overall agenda.

A Word about Counselling Students

I have found that participants in groups and seminars readily grasp the Six-Step Strategy and incorporate it with relative ease into their repertoire. Because their focus is self-development, they set to work on exploring their own experience with diligence. However, students engaged in learning to counsel others need extra guidance. Because their primary focus appears to be "What strategies can I learn that I can apply to others?", they may wish to forge ahead and put the strategy to use before they have understood its workings at first hand. Having seen this phenomenon in operation, I have found that it is important to insist that time be spent on exploring emotional experience vis-a-vis the self, before students of counselling can move on to use this strategy effectively to help others. If the work with self is done, and students experience first-hand how useful this strategy can be for unpacking the meanings in their emotional experience, they appear to acquire along the way an empathic sensitivity to the meanings and interpretations of others.

With Individuals

When I am working with individuals, the timing of the discussion that facilitates a shared understanding of feeling and emotion depends largely on how my client and I are working together.

If the client is there to work specifically with emotional difficulties, I may move directly into creating a shared understanding of emotional experience as part of the process of building our relationship. This allows us to work from common ground with regard to our approach to emotional experience, and facilitates the introduction of feeling as a way of knowing and the Six-Step Strategy as a possible self-help tool for the client.

Otherwise, I wait until we have begun to work on the client's experiences. Once feeling and emotion are very much in the forefront, I then introduce feeling as a way of knowing and the Six-Step Strategy in the following way. Having observed the client carefully for preferences in ways of knowing (see pp. 17-24, pp. 30-46 and pp. 49-50), I adjust my language and manner to reflect the client's. While reflecting the client's emotional experience, I begin asking questions that help to unpack the meanings of that experience. (See Key Questions for each step as outlined on pp. 93-96.)

If the client and I are still in the initial stages of exploring her experience, I may proceed only to Step Five, reflecting back the experience and communicating empathy until both the client and I are satisfied that I have a good grasp of what the experience means to her.

When the client has responded and expressed satisfaction with how we are proceeding, and it seems appropriate to move from relationship building and assessment to intervention, problem solving, and goal setting, I move to Step Six. I proceed to ask questions that help the client reframe her interpretations. If this works well over time, and the client begins to understand her experience in a different light, I suggest that she can learn to work with emotional experience by learning the Six Steps as a strategy that she can use whenever she chooses. At this point, I may also introduce ways of knowing as a framework for understanding self and others, and offer it to the client as another useful self-help tool. I have found that this psychoeducative approach to working with clients prepares them well for independence.

The Last Word

In the end, this strategy (or any other) succeeds or fails according to the assessment of those who have used it to help with their own experience. I will therefore leave the last word on feeling as a way of knowing to my clients and students.

Eighty percent of those to whom I have taught this approach to feeling and emotion (N=92) rated this as "very important" to their independent functioning. The other twenty percent rated it as "important." Although it was possible for all concerned to choose the categories "not important" or "marginally important," not a single individual in a three-year period has chosen either of these categories. One student summed it up this way:

> Until I learned that feeling is a way of knowing that helps me with what I'm experiencing, I thought that I was just overemotional. I thought that I was oversensitive and probably kind of childish because I had all these strong feelings all the time when I was supposed to be cool. But now I know that my feelings are actually telling me something important. They're telling me that I *know* something about what is going on, something that means something *to me,* that I can understand and learn from.

Another student said:

> Before learning about this, I put down my own feelings and other people's. I used to work hard to get rid of my emotions, and I was embarrassed that I wasn't more rational. I thought that the really intelligent people were probably those people who had their feelings under control and didn't let them get in the way. Now I realize that there is intelligence and knowledge in feeling. So, instead of pushing

my feelings away, I look more deeply into them to see what I can learn about myself.

Overall, students and clients have said again and again that what they find most helpful and useful about this approach is that they now no longer feel defensive about their feelings or overwhelmed by emotional experience. Because they can now relate to this aspect of human experience as interpretive work that they themselves have done, they find even their most difficult feelings valid and helpful instead of disruptive and intrusive.

References

Bard, P. (1934). The neurohumoral basis of emotional reactions. In Hutchison, C.A. (Ed.), *Handbook of general experimental psychology*. Worcester, MA: Clark University Press.

Beck, A.T. (1967). *Depression: Clinical, experimental and theoretical aspects*. New York: Harper & Row.

Belenky, M., Clinchy, B., Goldberger, N. & Tanile, J. (1986). *Women's ways of knowing*. New York: Basic Books.

Bowlby, J. (1988). *A secure base*. New York: Basic Books.

Buss, A. H. (1966). Instrumentality of aggression, feeedback, and frustration as determinants of physical aggression. *Journal of Personality & Social Psychology, 3*, 153-162.

Cannon, W.B. (1927). *The pleasure areas*. London: Eyre Methuen.

Corey, G. (1991). *The theory and practice of counselling and psychotherapy*. Pacific Grove, CA: Brooks Cole.

Davison, G.C. & Neale, J.M. (1982). *Abnormal psychology*, 3rd edition. New York: John Wiley & Sons.

de Sousa, R. (1990). *The rationality of emotion*. Cambridge, MA: MIT Press.

Durant, W. (1926). *The story of philosophy*. Englewood Cliffs, NJ: Prentice-Hall.

Ellis, A. (1988). *How to stubbornly refuse to make yourself miserable about anything, yes anything*. Secaucus, NJ: Lyle Stuart.

Gadamer, H.G. (1992). *Truth and method*. New York: Crossroad.

Gilligan, C. (1982). *In a different voice: Psychological theory and moral development*. Cambridge, MA: Harvard University Press.

Heidbieder, E. (1961). *Seven psychologies*. Englewood Cliffs, NJ: Prentice-Hall.

Humboldt, W. (1967). In Edwards (Ed.), *The encyclopedia of philosophy*. New York: Collier MacMillan.

Jung, C. (1928). *The structure and dynamics of the psyche*. Translated by R.T.C. Hull. Princeton, NJ: Princeton University Press.

Loew, C.A. (1967). Acquisition of a hostile attitude and its relationship to behavior. *Journal of Personality & Social Psychology, 5*, 335-341.

Lyons, N. (1988). Two perspectives: On self, relationships, and morality. In C. Gilligan, J. Ward, J. Taylor, and B. Bardige (Eds.), *Mapping the moral domain*. Cambridge, MA: Harvard University Press.

Mahoney, M.J. (1991). *Human change processes: The scientific foundations of psychotherapy*. New York: Basic Books.

Nelsen, E.A. (1969). Social reinforcement for expression vs. suppression of aggression. *Merrill-Palmer Quarterly of Behavior & Development, 15*, 259-278.

Odle, U. (1990). *Practical visualization*. Glasgow: Wm. Collins & Sons.

Peale, N.V. (1982). *Dynamic imaging, the powerful way to change*. Old Tappan, NJ: Revell.

Peavy, R.V. (1977). *Empathic listening workbook*. Victoria, BC: Adult Counselling Project, University of Victoria.

Peavy, R.V. (in press). *Constructive career counselling: A practical guidebook for counsellors*. Toronto: Trifolium Books.

Pelletier, K. (1977). *Mind as healer, mind as slayer*. New York: Delta.

Rossi, E. (1986). *The psychology of mind-body healing*. New York: W.W. Norton.

Rush, A.J., Beck, A.T., Kovacs, M., & Hollow, S.D. (1977). Comparative efficacy of cognitive therapy and pharmaco-therapy in the treatment of depressed outpatients. *Cognitive Therapy & Research, 1*, 17-39.

Schachter, S. & Singer, J.E. (1962). Cognitive social and physiological determinants of emotional state. *Psychological Review, 69*, 379-399.

Schmale, A.H. & Iker, H. (1971). Hopelessness as a prediction of cervical cancer. *Social Science Medicine, 5*, 95-100.

Seligman, M.E.P. (1975). *Helplessness: On depression, development and death*. San Francisco: Freeman.

Simonton, O. & Simonton, S. (1978). *Getting well again*. Los Angeles: St. Martin's Press.

Singer, J. & Loomis, M. (1984). *Interpretive guide for the Singer Loomis Inventory of Personality*. Palo Alto, CA: Consulting Psychologists Press.

Solomon, R. (1983). *The passions: The myth and nature of the human emotions*. Notre Dame, IN: University of Notre Dame Press.

Vaihinger, H. (1924) [1911]. *The philosophy of "as if"*. Berlin: Reuther & Reichard.

von Glaserfeld, E. (1984). *An introduction to radical constructivism*. New York: W.W. Norton.

Webster's encyclopedic dictionary. (1988). New York: Lexicon.

Webster's new collegiate dictionary (1975). Springfield, MA: Merriam.

Index